your
lifebuilder

ride the vision
of your life

your
lifebuilder

e dan smith

SPIRAL RANCH

Boulder, Colorado

©2002 by Spiral Ranch

Spiral Ranch, P.O. Box 19726, Boulder, CO 80308-2726
www.yourlifebuilder.com

Editor: Nancy E. Levin
Design: Amy Hayes | Origin

A CIP Catalog Record for this book is available from the
Library of Congress.

ISBN 0-9719761-0-4

Dedication

To the memory of my mother, Judith Gray Walton Smith—whose legacy lives on through the strong women that she left with me: her mother—Hautense Walton, my wife—Kate, and my children—Eliza and Ava.

Contents

Acknowledgments

Throughout this project people appeared out of thin air—like angels—encouraging me to move forward when I did not even know what or where forward meant. I thank them all from the bottom of my heart.

To Elizabeth Sargent, for immediately encouraging me to do something with my *LifeBuilder*. Without her insight and belief in me, *Your LifeBuilder* would have been incomplete.

To Curtis Estes, for believing in my message from the beginning, brainstorming with me, and inviting me to speak about LifeBuilder for the first time.

To Scott Richards, for providing me true support during the writing process. Our friendship is a blessing.

To Kenlyn Kolleen, for telling more people about this project than anyone else alive and for joining the first LifeBuilder group and giving it the "Edge" factor.

To my editor Nancy Levin, for taking the rawness of the manuscript and giving it the proper form and structure, while keeping the message intact—whose ability to simultaneously smile, laugh, and give matter-of-fact critical advice is perfect for what she does.

To Amy Hayes, for her graphic design expertise. Her ability to create a compelling book cover and interior design without any real art direction from me continues to amaze and impress.

To Wendy Keller, for responding to my initial query with tremendous enthusiasm. Without her, this book would never have seen the light of day.

To Tom Richards, Brian Cunningham and everyone in the Northwestern Mutual family, whose incredible dedication to and belief in their mission has inspired me many times.

To Bud and Nancy, Minnie Bell, Mark Schoofs, John Devore, John Clancy, Brucie and Greg, Parker Johnson, Philip Tirone, John Hunt, Tina Armstrong, Randy Roark, Clinton McKinzie, Joseph A. De Nucci, Sky Canyon, Paul Wallace, the 5, David Rich, Alex Goulden, Corey Nakai, Brett Conrad, George Smith, Blair Green, Kent Sims, Sarah Chesnutt and anyone else I have forgotten to mention who has supported me in the process of creating and completing this book.

To Sally, Sully and Max, for moving to Boulder and graciously extending their love and belief in me, and for helping us immeasurably as we finalized this project.

To my Grandmother, for supporting me emotionally, financially and matter-of-factly in times of need without asking too many questions; and who has become much more than a grandmother since my mother died in 1986.

To my father, who gave me encouragement exactly when I needed it, for always being unbelievably supportive of me, for setting a new standard in our family for personal growth and for passing on the gift of writing and spiritual depth—I am forever grateful.

To my brother Alden and sister Elizabeth, for supporting me more than they could ever realize.

To my two children, Eliza and Ava, for running to the door every day when I come home to take me away to places that I remember from long ago; for letting me read them books, play games, laugh, tickle, and love them by being completely themselves in the moment of now—the way children ought to be. I am so grateful to have so much energy and love in my home.

And finally, to my life partner and soul mate Kate; whose partnership has allowed just the right amount of space to grow without falling too far; whose spiritual quest and dedication to being fully alive in herself as mother, friend, partner, and writer is inspirational and genius; whose willingness to place her professional life on hold to raise the children at home is to be forever appreciated; and to whom I am fully committed with every fiber of my being—I will be forever grateful.

Thank you all.

Approaching
the Gateway

*As you express, project, and act upon
your authentic intentions, a plan for the life you
were meant to live will unfold to support you
in every conceivable way—and no matter
what, you cannot fail.*

Walking down the road with a
budding photographer on the way
to a photo shoot, I asked,

"What kind of life
do you want to have?
What are your dreams?"

"WHATEVER LIFESTYLE THIS CAREER GIVES ME," was his sheepish reply, holding up his camera to look at it as if it held the answer. "Someday I'd like to work photography full-time, in the studio—I guess."

Sensing that he felt incapable to truly have an effect on such things, that he was destined to just whimsically bump along in life, I gently challenged him, "Do you think it works that way, or do you think that you have a hand in how things turn out?"

"What do you mean?"

"What if you took the lifestyle you really wanted—one that embodies the true essence of you—and expressed it in pictures, symbols, and words, and then looked at that expression every day? By simply projecting this vision into the Universe, you would attract the right kind of work, life experiences, and relationships to allow you to live an authentic expression of that vision!"

"I don't really know...."

Silence.

"Do you really think it works that way?," he asked with a good bit of skepticism.

"How else could it possibly work?" I responded.

My hope is that you were drawn to this book because you heard it whisper, "This is *Your LifeBuilder*," and you felt intrigued to pick it up because you could sense that this was no ordinary self-help book and that it contained something—anything!—to put you back in touch with the essence of a life worth living.

And, in fact, it is far different than any other book you have bought. Like me, you may have bought hundreds of books and tapes over the years in an effort to improve the circumstances of your life (or this could be your first one!)—whether you wanted to lose weight, become wealthy, improve your relationships, release old patterns of behavior, or find your life's purpose. Or perhaps for the first time you are sensing that the road you have chosen does not lead anywhere that you want to be.

What is unique about *Your LifeBuilder*, is that it will guide you to create a book called *your* **LifeBuilder**.

Your LifeBuilder is a simple ten-to-fifteen-page book containing the most important goals and intentions of your life, linked to inspiring images and photographs of people, places, and things you are passionate about. The primary component of your LifeBuilder is your New Life Vision—a masterful projection of your best-imaged life. The rest of your LifeBuilder is comprised of supporting pages that are places to collect prayers, your best ideas, as well as the wisdom and knowledge received from the great thinkers and teachers through the ages.

Creating your LifeBuilder will put you in touch with the electrifying power of spiritual co-creation to manifest powerful changes in your life, revealing your authenticity. As your life begins to shift, your LifeBuilder unfolds right along with you, continuously reflecting and manifesting the life of your updated dreams.

The way this process came about is that I, like you, have been on a personal crusade to make my life better for many years. I began to notice a common thread of wisdom in all of the self-help books I was reading—*your thoughts create your reality, follow your heart—it will guide you, and there is a life purpose specifically for you somewhere out there.*

I knew all those things, but I was still too paralyzed by fear, negative emotion, and indecision to integrate any of it. My excuse was that I was already too busy in my life to make it stick. So I would find my notes from a seminar or from the latest self-help book somewhere in the bottom of the pile on my desk three months after I had promised to incorporate them into my life—and I then would get pumped up again. I kept finding myself in an unhealthy cycle of being inspired and then uninspired, over and over again, without any lasting change.

How many times have you felt frustrated like this?

Finally, taking my life into my own hands, I made **my** LifeBuilder book, and soon found myself blowing through my fears. I had discovered a new passion for life—a passion that was far more sustained and authentic than the fleeting moments of inspiration I was accustomed to. It was through this new passion that I discovered an authentic New Life Vision—and my desire to share my experiences with you.

In the chapters that follow, I will illustrate the tried and proven process of creating a LifeBuilder book and developing a simple supporting practice or ritual.

The results of this will be immeasurable to you.

I had never even considered the idea of writing a book, but one day I could do nothing else but write this book and think of ways to help people through LifeBuilder. While logically I should have stuck with my old life—it was in fact, providing a pretty good lifestyle—my LifeBuilder was making it alarmingly clear that the lifestyle was not authentically representative of who I am. I became aware of my own intuitive voice and truly felt better, from a place deep inside, when I was writing. The voice kept telling me, "Write the book—write the book."

And so I wrote the book and somehow everything I needed was provided for me—money, ideas, space, an editor, a publicist, and investors. In fact, everything else in my life got better and better too, including the relationships with my family and friends as I began to live a life rooted in my authenticity.

I owe all of this to **my** LifeBuilder.

This book is my story, and while you may find yourself living a bit more of my life than you would like, I speak intimately with you so you can understand the process. I will, however, sprinkle in stories of some of the many other people who have been using LifeBuilder in their lives to give you the benefit of perspective.

I suspect that this book has found its way into your hands for good reason. It will take you on a unique journey of self-expression and projection, which will naturally propel you into the corresponding supporting activities—a cyclical process necessary for moving through your challenges into an authentic life experience.

I now dedicate this book to YOU and *YOUR* LifeBuilder.

First you will **express** a New Life Vision—including creating new supportive thinking and identifying old limiting thoughts and beliefs currently standing in your way—by using a creative format. Something magical happens the minute you do this.

Secondly, you will **project** this new line of thinking into the Universe through your daily interaction with your LifeBuilder, replacing your old thinking by anchoring new thoughts with positive emotional associations.

This will propel you into **action**! Infused with the energy of your New Life Vision, you will create change and manifest a new life experience without strain or struggle.

Now it is time to be real.

Accept the challenge and ride into the life you are meant to live by setting the following intention:

I choose to consciously engage in the co-creation of my life, authentically and intentionally attracting everything I desire spiritually, physically, and materially.

X _____ Date _____

Read Chapter One ONLY after you sign above.

How to Use This Book

Each chapter of the book is followed by exercises. These exercises yield the actual pages for your LifeBuilder book.

There are two ways to approach this book:

As recommended—Read each chapter and then complete the exercises at the end of each chapter in a sequential fashion before moving on, taking the necessary time to complete them.

Your way—Read a few chapters to get an idea of the flow of the book and then figure out what works for you. You might return to the exercises after finishing the book, or simply take the book for what it is worth.

Once you decide to create your LifeBuilder book, then start the exercises at the end of each chapter. It is essential that you complete them in a sequential order. I highly suggest that you do these exercises when you are feeling good—after exercise or mediation, when your thinking is positive and clear.

In the back of this book there are perforated pages to record the results of these exercises for your LifeBuilder pages. As you work through the book, tear these pages out and keep them together. In Chapter Seven, you are going to assemble Your LifeBuilder book using these pages.

You will want to have a container (your LifeBuilder book) to assemble your LifeBuilder before you finish Chapter Six.

There are two options for this:

Go to or call any office supply store and purchase a binder with at least 15 clear presentation-style pages—these pages are made of clear plastic for 8.5" x 11" sheets of paper that allow you to slip the pages in so that you can see the front and back.

OR

Contact us. We have designed specific LifeBuilder book containers that are available on our website, www.yourlifebuilder.com or through our toll-free ordering service, 1-877-SPIRAL1 (1-877-774-7251). These LifeBuilder books simplify both the assembly of your LifeBuilder and your daily practice, and contain easy-to-use templates for creating your LifeBuilder pages.

Our commitment is to give you as much assistance as we can. For a wealth of free information and products that can lend a hand in the process, please visit the website and click on *LifeBuilder Help*.

Good Luck!

chapter one

Setting
the Intention

"Do the thing and you will have the power."
— RALPH WALDO EMERSON

Have you ever been in the flow, as if everything seemed to be going your way?

PERHAPS YOU STARTED A NEW BUSINESS or a new job and it seems like everything is running along a predetermined script. You are coincidently meeting the right people at exactly the right moments, saying the right things and making good decisions. New customers and opportunities appear seemingly out of thin air. Every time you need money to expand the business or reach a sales goal, you seem to close a deal worth that amount of money. You are even making all the green lights and finding all the right parking spaces!

What is really happening to connect all the dots?

It is your willingness to set a clear intention, remaining true to yourself and open to possibility.

In 2000, I was living in Pennsylvania. My wife, Kate, and I had just bought a home and had our second child. Her parents, sister, brother, and our nephew lived close by. I had just started a new career on a commission-only basis in the life insurance business and every nickel we had was locked up in the deposit on our new home with little to spare.

The time in Pennsylvania became very difficult for us. We felt as though we were stuck in the mud and at the mercy of some great conspiracy to keep us broke and unhappy—we were not in the flow. Although I had two beautiful children and the best wife I could ever have hoped for, I spent a great deal of my time angry and frustrated. I was not much fun to be around and noticed that my attitude was rubbing off on my children—this I could not bear to watch. My days at the office consisted mostly of just staring at the phone, waiting for my attitude to change. I was scared, confused, and doing everything to avoid building my business and improving my life. It seemed like nothing could go my way, even though I knew that I held the keys to changing my experience.

Just one month earlier, I had attended an inspiring and exciting regional sales convention in New York, and left with every intention to apply what I had learned in order to make a great success of my life.

As soon as I returned home, my promise quickly faded and I became despondent again, staring at the phone and meeting with people who did not seem to appreciate my services, and then dragging myself through the motions of my family life. I knew what I needed to do but I just couldn't seem to get motivated.

Have you ever felt this way?

"Wouldn't it be great if I could bottle the enthusiasm of that convention and uncork it any time I need a lift?" I thought to myself as I flipped through a magazine. I turned to a two-page advertisement with a magnificent mountain range in the background. The photograph resonated with me, and I let myself imagine how wonderful it would be to be there right now. I imagined that these were the Colorado mountains—and I reflected back to when I had lived there a few years before. I thought to myself, "I will look at this photograph every day for inspiration, and perhaps it will encourage me to appreciate my life more, motivate me to perform my job more effectively, be a better father, and make enough money to afford a vacation in Colorado!"

I carefully placed this photograph on the cover of my sales journal so that I would look at it on a daily basis when I recorded my daily sales activity before leaving the office.

The significance of this one simple action and the corresponding habit of looking at the photograph every day did not become immediately clear to me, but some unusual things began to happen.

My wife, Kate, and I began seriously talking about going to Colorado on vacation. Just a few weeks before, we had dismissed this as impossibility because of our very young children and no solid income. Now, we were suddenly figuring out how to make it work with what we had. We began to see that the antidote to our stagnation was to go on vacation to a place we were passionate about and truly take the time to rest, relax, and dream again, rather than sit around in our misery. Even though the trip cost more money than we had in the bank, we went!

Before the plane even landed in Colorado, Kate stunned both of us by stating emphatically what we were both suddenly and silently thinking, "Honey, let's move to Colorado!" Until this instant, leaving her hometown or her family was not even a distant possibility for either one of us!

It took the balance of the week in Colorado to explore what we were both feeling. When we returned from our vacation, we took one look at the life we had been silently and unhappily living and decided to explore our options. Instead of feeling trapped by our circumstances, we were inspired by new possibility. Nothing had changed except for our attitudes and we were filled with a passion that opened our eyes to a brand new perspective.

I called my company's regional agency manager in Boulder, Colorado, and scheduled a meeting for two weeks later and bought plane tickets for my family. Boulder provided the community we wanted to be a part of and the company's office seemed like a great environment in which to build a successful career. The trip was a success and I was offered the last available office they had, and they were even willing to pay for our moving expenses.

We made the decision to move right then and there, provided we could hurdle the large obstacles in our way. All our money was tied up in the house we had just purchased and it had sat on the market for eight months before we bought it.

What did we have to lose? It was if some great new energy had invigorated us, and so upon returning to Pennsylvania on a Tuesday morning, we put our house up for sale that afternoon. By Saturday, we had a full price offer and the new buyers wanted to move in exactly the same time we wanted to move out. Needless to say we accepted their offer and were on our way to Boulder.

Now we were really in the flow!

On my first day of work in Boulder, I was anxious to get started. I tried to move into my new office—but it had become the graveyard for every squeaky chair, broken phone and old filing cabinet for the entire company—there was nowhere to work! Frustrated, I walked out into the hall and tried to figure out who I needed to talk to about the situation.

The view of the Colorado Mountains out my window was the exact replica of the photo on my sales journal!

At that very moment, down at the other end of the hallway on the other side of the building, a four-year insurance agent had just decided to quit the company, leaving one of the most desirable offices available. Fate was being generous with me.

That afternoon he moved out and I moved in.

Excited about my new digs, I sat down at my desk for the first time with scattered files and half-unpacked boxes all around me. Surveying the view of the mountains to the west out my new window, I suddenly realized I had seen this very view before, and yet that was the first time I was ever physically there. This was a déja-vu of monumental proportions!

It was if I had just walked directly into the scene of my dreams.

I ransacked one of the boxes on the floor, searching for my sales journal. Quickly finding it, I opened to the page I had seen so many times before. The picture I had torn from a magazine—that I had been coveting all this time—was the same view now outside my new office window. The view of the Colorado mountains out my window was the exact replica of the photo on my sales journal! I held it out in front of me, comparing the picture with the actual view. Down to the last detail they were unbelievably alike, even the trees were in similar places. "How could this be?" I thought, as I sat there in amazement, trying to grasp the magnitude of the moment.

It was then that I realized the very act of placing the photograph of the mountains in my sales journal months earlier and looking at it daily, was the catalyst for change. It had caused me to speak differently to Kate about the Colorado vacation that ultimately led to her voicing our collective desire to move there. The rest of the details unfolded naturally one step at a time, without strain or struggle—including finding a new home, getting a new mortgage, closing enough business to keep our cash flow going, and culminating with the right office becoming available on my first day of work!

Unbelievable! But here I was.

Still vibrating from this experience and acutely aware of having tapped into a new power source, I walked down the hall and asked someone whom I had just met to come to my office so I could explain what had just happened. After I told him the story I just told you, the question had to be asked, "Wow! If this can happen to me by just looking at one picture; what would happen if I created a whole book of images around the most important goals of my life?"

And so began a new life experience.

I then built my first LifeBuilder. It was about ten pages long and filled with photographs and images representing the life I wanted to live. I put affirmations next to the photographs and included a mission statement for my business as well as my sales language. I also included inspirational quotes and ideas I gleaned from reading books and attending seminars. I placed sales goals and income goals there. It was loosely organized at first, but uniquely mine and very powerful.

I committed myself to begin each day by looking at my LifeBuilder. This "commitment" was fun! I got to start every day knowing that what I was looking at in my LifeBuilder was soon going to be in my life! I made it so cool that I actually felt compelled to pick it up. This created inspirational accountability—it had its own energy, calling to me from my desktop every morning. I became intimately familiar with the contents and kept refining the material that I placed in my LifeBuilder, and the most amazing things began to happen—not only did I discover a true passion for my work that I never knew I was capable of, but my income increased dramatically due to my new enthusiasm for sales! Best of all, I felt fantastic inside and everyone in my life was positively affected by my new optimistic attitude. Life seemed to be opening up for me in every way.

In nine months time, despite moving to a new town with limited prior sales success, I became a leading life insurance producer in my national peer group for one of the largest, most prominent life insurance companies in the country! My life was a complete turnaround from what it had been before I had put the picture of the mountains on my sales journal. Quite simply, none of this could ever have happened in my previous state of mind.

So how did simply looking at the photo of the mountains, and then ultimately my LifeBuilder book—filled with a visual representation of the life I wanted to live—help me make all these changes?

The mountains became a symbol of my intention to live a better life.

First, I had expressed the intention of making a great success of my life using a visual and emotional anchor—the mountain picture. The desire to change my life was intense, and the mountains were something that spoke directly to my soul—they represented freedom to me. It was this image, embedded in my mind and attached to my desire for a better life, that caused my thinking and awareness to shift. Once I set that intention, life took off! I stopped focusing on what I did not want and made the space for what I desired to bring into my life.

Furthermore, the images that I subsequently placed in my new LifeBuilder were also images that spoke directly to the essence of who I was and wanted to become—these images were of things I was passionate about—my family, surfing, hiking, etc.—and were absolutely stunning.

The mountains became a symbol of my intention to live a better life.

Second, I discovered that there was great power in the habit of looking at my LifeBuilder on a daily basis. I was not just looking at my book—I was living it. For that short amount of time, early in the morning, I was getting so excited about the New Life Vision I had expressed with bright colored images and words that it was affecting the energy vibration I carried into each day.

This energy vibration was the key to my dramatic increase in sales and my new optimistic attitude. It was this energy that opened my subconscious mind to embrace a new line of thought.

What I discovered was that I had, in essence, created my own life-advertising program. By employing the same techniques that any advertiser would use in trying to influence me to buy their product, I advertised my best life to myself every day

This book is about taking one action and developing one simple habit that will change your thinking at a deep level, allowing you to follow through on your authentic intentions for living a more fulfilling life!

and it had helped me change my thinking, my attitude, and my entire life!

However, this was far superior to just any ordinary advertisement—I had tapped into something mystical and spiritual that I could not logically explain. This was a fantastic gift because it engaged me in the creative process of uncovering my inherent authentic self. Through creating a more conscious connection to Spirit, I discovered a life purpose I never knew existed. I had accessed something far beyond what I could have ever seen for myself before, and I soon found myself being guided to new goals. I had the courage to move through my fears into a new life experience in a creative and dynamic way.

Changing our thinking is a major key to changing our lives. Our thinking is what links us to powerful emotions that either bind us or release us. We each possess the power necessary to support this change, but too often we are unable to follow through because we have not found a methodology that inspires us to stay with the commitment that must be made. And yet the key to making this change is all around us. We experience advertising repeatedly every day. All we need to do is take this tried and true process and apply it to ourselves consciously.

This book is about taking **one action** and developing **one simple habit** that will change your thinking at a deep level, allowing you to follow through on your authentic intentions for living a more fulfilling life!

The **one action** you can take now is to develop your LifeBuilder! Take the highest vision of life you can imagine and organize it into your own fantastic self-directed life-advertising program, using inspiring images, artwork, objects, and writing.

By completing the assignments at the end of each chapter, you will be holding your LifeBuilder in your hands as soon as you finish this book.

The **one habit** is to start each day with the practice of completely immersing yourself in your LifeBuilder to generate supportive energy and a new perspective. This can be done in as few as ten minutes. Toward the end of this book, you will naturally be inspired to easily incorporate this simple routine into your life.

Most of us make a mad dash into our days, negatively influenced by the outside world through the newspaper, radio, television, and especially other people. I encourage you to dedicate at least ten minutes at the beginning of your day to reviewing your LifeBuilder book. By spending this time with your LifeBuilder, rather than with reports of what has occurred in the past or what you fear may happen in the future, you will set the tone necessary to make new changes. The extent of this interaction will govern the depth and permanence of growth you will experience. Reading your LifeBuilder is a daily ritual that when partnered with a spiritual practice—such as a traditional religion, prayer, meditation, yoga, writing, etc.—can become even more powerful on your journey of change.

What started as a whimsical act of tearing out a magazine advertisement developed into an incredible journey of self-actualization beyond any of my wildest imaginings, including a great desire to share *LifeBuilder* with you.

The next five chapters highlight stages of my life chronologically, during which I learned valuable lessons. Each of these lessons build on one another and will help you better understand *Your LifeBuilder*.

The Power of Authenticity

Naturally, our peers, parents, and culture have influenced us to live in accordance with what others expect of us, which is not necessarily the way we're meant to live. The key to creating the life we want is to connect to the true essence of who we are but have been afraid to express. As we begin to bring our New Life Vision into creative form, we force ourselves to be aware of the parts of our lives that are authentic, and those that are not. The energy that we used to put into self-created drama will now be redirected into the creation of a New Life Vision.

Underground Thinking

Our life experiences are directly related to our mind's thinking pattern that was partially developed during our childhood. By understanding that this subconscious level of thinking, or underground thinking, creates our reality, we realize that we must now take personal conscious responsibility for what we think and believe. We must ultimately bring our thinking into harmony with our authenticity—giving us more personal power.

The Power of a New Life Vision

The mind works for us when we give it a focus—this has been proven over and over again. Intelligent goal setting is successful in ways that may be difficult to grasp, but are undeniable all the same. By expressing our best authentic intentions through a creative, visually stimulating process, we engage more fully with the power of our minds, allowing for us to be energetically pulled into a new life experience.

Advertising works!

Madison Avenue utilizes tried and true ways of accessing our minds to influence our thinking regarding purchasing decisions. We can apply these effective, successful techniques on ourselves by anchoring new thinking in our minds, which will naturally and effortlessly begin to change our behavior and then our lives.

Spirit Is Higher Than Intellect

Through the creative elements of your LifeBuilder book and the ensuing process of active surrender to your LifeBuilder practice, we find new areas of authentic expression and truth opening us up to a new life experience that is even better than the one we had imagined before. Exponential and expansive growth occurs as we move deeper into the spiritual realm by uncovering and releasing our attachments without effort or strain. We naturally learn to accept ourselves, exactly as we are and where we are, as we look out at what we want to co-create for the future.

You are holding the power to change your life in your hands.

The key is simply to follow through with purpose. Make a statement and let it all hang out—fully integrating your individuality with everything else that you have read and learned that resonates with your being about the life experience you want for yourself—know no boundaries. Put your ideas here first, and use others' ideas only in a supporting role. This is the place to capture your intuitive voice.

I have written this book from an inclusive perspective so that people from every religion and spiritual tradition, as well as those without any, can participate in the process. While I believe deeply in my definition of Spirit and the Universe, your LifeBuilder is a way for you to extract and record what you believe in order to formulate your own life philosophy, and then open-mindedly live it your way. I will also refer to a master plan or blueprint for life—this can be simply equated to you being the absolute best person you can be, or falling in-line with God's plan for your life. Please feel free to substitute any concept you would like. Regardless of what I believe, your ability to live the life you desire is tied to your commitment of consistently following your heart and no one else's. Deeply knowing that you are not dependent upon the wisdom of others, but instead that you are living interdependently with the world around you, will keep you inspired.

In advance, let me share with you two of the obstacles you may face.

First of all, putting together your LifeBuilder may be a significant challenge.

What seems like an easy task may cause you to examine your life in such a way that may make you feel uneasy. Facing the truth of the life we have created up until now can be a terrifying experience.

Secondly, as you move into your LifeBuilder practice, the "who" you think you are now is most likely not the person you will get to know as you move forward. Again this can be an unsettling proposition. Most amazingly, this discovery will lead you to a deepening relationship with your true self and serve as the gateway necessary for you to pass through in order to experience the life you desire. The antidote is to take plenty of time and space during the transition process. Following the guidelines set forth in this book has the power to change your life completely by releasing exciting, vital energy inside of you.

Most great things in life seem to come to us quite by accident and through a sequence of seemingly unconnected and mysterious events, and they can hardly be explained as they are happening. When we look back later though, we can see how everything came together through a combination of setting our most authentic intentions and then letting go. As hard as we try to explain these away as random occurrences and continue to try and control the details of our lives, we observe that the secret lies in embracing ourselves as integral parts of a greater whole.

We each have access to the power of the Universe. We can either choose to live and work consciously with this power or we can live our lives unconsciously. Your LifeBuilder is designed to embody the conscious realization of that power as it connects you to the life you want to live.

I wish you well on your journey.

CHAPTER ONE

EXERCISES

Design or find your symbol
for a better life!

Exercise 1-1

Below, design or place a symbol for your intention to create a new life experience. The mountains were my original symbol. You may want to use something already in your life or find something completely new. You may already know what this symbol is—it may have come to you in a dream. You may leaf through magazines or surf the Internet. Whatever you use, personalize it. Place your creative stamp on it to make it yours.

This symbol will become your logo—a visual representation of your intention to improve your life and the corresponding New Life Vision. This logo will come to symbolize your best intentions by immediately bringing to mind all of the contents of your LifeBuilder at a single glance.

EXERCISES continued

Exercise 1-2

As you will discover, your LifeBuilder will include many images, ideas, and words; forms of artwork and color; photographs, and other creative material.

Become aware as you are reading magazines or books of the material that you would like to use to express your new life experience. Cut or copy these and keep them in the pocket of your LifeBuilder book with your perforated LifeBuilder pages. For further direction, please read the instructions for Exercise 5-2 on page 79.

LIFEBUILDER ACTION # 1

My New Life Symbol. Tear out perforated page #1 from the back of the book. Place your symbol on that page. Make copies of your symbol. Place others on your desk at work, the rearview mirror of your car, on your refrigerator, or scan it into your computer for wallpaper, or put it on your favorite coffee mug. Your mind will immediately reference your deep desire to live authentically just by seeing your symbol. Keep this perforated page and other images for your LifeBuilder in a safe place, or in your LifeBuilder book. On our website, www.yourlifebuilder.com, there is a wealth of free information including a free LifeBuilder template to download as a substitute for the perforated pages. These will be 8 1/2" x 11" — the same size as your LifeBuilder.

The Power of Authenticity

"When you are content to be simply yourself and don't compare or compete, everybody will respect you."

— LAO-TZU
CHINESE PHILOSOPHER

In the title of their
enormously popular
rock-n-roll song,
The Who raises the
always-important
question: "Who **are** you?"

WELL, WHO ARE YOU? Are you living true to yourself, or are you consumed with what you are—an attorney, a mother, a dreamer, a student, or an athlete?

Do you know how you came to the life you are living?

_____

In order to fully illustrate the powerful changes I have experienced in my life, I need to take you back to the beginning.

On a glorious and crisp afternoon in the fall of 1989, driving down the interstate with my friend Jenny, I thought honestly about who I was for the first time in my life. At 21 years old, I had recently graduated college and had just returned from a backpacking trip—the reality of having to make some hard decisions about how I was going to support myself were staring me in the face. As each mile marker passed, my freedom seemed to be coming closer to an end.

Jenny had just finished telling me about how she had made up her mind to take an overseas Peace Corps position, when she asked me:

"What are you going to do with your life?"

"I am going back to Nashville to get into the life insurance business with my father and grandfather," I said.

The answer just rolled off my tongue, an automatic response, without any thinking and certainly no emotion. I had never seriously considered doing anything else. All of my relatives lived right down the street from where I grew up and I just assumed that's what the Smiths did. I was so numb to who I was, completely unaware that I had a choice.

She instantly became aware that I was not in touch with myself and asked, "No, what do you really want to do?"

No one had ever asked me this question demanding such a sincere response. I was startled and felt exposed, but I knew that another unconscious answer was not going to work. I stalled, relieved that the road demanded my eye contact.

All the statements I had been hearing for years and years were suddenly circling in my mind:

"Life insurance is in your blood—you are a natural."

"When are you going to join the company?"

"I bet you're going to follow in the footsteps of your father and grandfather, aren't you?"

Somehow these seemed to have little relevance right now, and I was suddenly aware of other desires I had been suppressing to give into what was expected of me.

"You mean ... what do I really want to do?"

Her silence was deafening, and there was nothing but the unanswered question and another 150 miles of highway ahead as I pondered this idea.

The answer suddenly came to me! Surprised, I responded, "What I would really like to do is to go out west and open an outside expedition business in the Colorado mountains."

I had often dreamed of one day going to live in Colorado. However, every time I thought about what I would have to let go of to go there, I buried that dream by telling myself, "I can't do that, it's irresponsible! I have to get into the life insurance business."

"Well, why not do it then?" Jenny asked, followed by a lot more silence.

Before this very moment, I was unconsciously living life according to others' ideals. It didn't take long to realize that I had been caught up in this for my entire life—disregarding what I wanted to do and doing what was expected of me. People were forever asking me, "What are you going to do with the rest of your life?" Unsure about myself and a little annoyed with the persistent questioning, I started answering with statements that got supportive responses. Since the Nashville-based insurance salesman answer received universal acceptance, I gave in.

It is easy for anyone just to go along with what is expected of him.

It is easy for anyone just to go along with what is expected of him, like this. Maybe you have done it yourself....

In the car with Jenny, I suddenly caught a glimpse of a brilliant ray of light I had never allowed myself to see before. It was too beautiful to ignore and too far away to recognize completely, and I knew that I had to make a conscious, significant decision—there was no turning back this time.

I could finally see beyond the one road straight ahead, my life began to open up with endless possibilities and I felt energized. I realized that all those people encouraging me to stay in Nashville could not possibly know what was best for me, and that what they were saying was only a reflection of what they wanted—not what I wanted. And, feeling the weight of the family's expectations, I had overlooked myself.

Jenny questioning me was not coincidental. There was a place inside of me that was truly disconcerted with settling for the illusionary hope of safety and predictability. Clearly seeing that I was disconnected from my dreams and my heart's desire, she had the wisdom to pull the truth out of me. She was not from Nashville and had no attachment to me being anywhere—she only wanted to help me see what was best for me, and follow my heart.

"I am going to do it!" I told her. Right then and there the commitment was made.

My heart led me to Colorado—where I opened a bike and snowboard adventure store after borrowing $5,000 from my grandfather. I just happened to meet someone else at exactly the right time with a similar dream and we became partners. We built a successful business together, experiencing great growth and excitement at work in the mountains. I met my wife Kate soon after and immediately knew that she was my life partner. I was on a true path of self-development. All the wonderful things that happened to me during this phase of life—my wife, my children, great ideas for business and personal growth—came to me without any struggle or resistance. I was in the flow, discovering that one authentic action led to another.

So what had really happened? How had I suddenly gone from being obligated to the Nashville insurance life to live the life I truly wanted?

First of all, being with Jenny provided a forum for expressing my authentic desires and intentions. Had I not ended up in that situation, I would have continued suppressing that desire—expressing that desire was the catalyst.

You may not have a Jenny—but you do have LifeBuilder! Use this resource as your own sounding board to take the important first step.

Second, I created a desirable lifestyle in my mind that was more compelling than staying in Nashville. I had, just for a moment, felt what it would be like to follow my heart—and this was strong enough to propel me through my fears. I focused on that vision rather than the difficulty of leaving. At that stage of my life, I did it unconsciously; you can use your LifeBuilder to do this consciously and more effectively.

When I think about how my life would have been if I stayed in Nashville, I know that my experience would have been largely inauthentic and ruled by "I should." Deep regret from "going through the motions" would have naturally followed. "I should" had been the reference point of my decision-making up until then. Continuing to make decisions from that place would have kept me "out of the flow." I would have followed through with a predictable series of decisions and would have always regretted what would have naturally followed—the job I would have taken, the person I would have married, the home I would have bought, and the person I would have become.

Change doesn't have to include a geographical move nor is there anything wrong with Nashville of course! But we all have a *Nashville* (any strong cultural influence—a town, a family, a relationship, a career, an inner belief system, a clique of friends, or any of these combined) that we use to overlook what we truly desire, settling for the status quo because everyone else seems to be making it work just fine.

Perhaps you are in what others define as the "perfect" relationship—everybody else thinks it's wonderful but secretly you are unfulfilled. Since you are not sure you could find anyone better, and you certainly do not want to disrupt your other relationships, you stay. Or no one from your family or neighborhood has ever done what you are secretly aspiring to do. Or, perhaps like all of your siblings, you work in the successful family business. You really want to start your own restaurant but you're too afraid to tell anyone in the event that you will appear ungrateful for your good fortune. Or maybe you are majoring in business when you really want to study theater, but your parents continuously exclaim that they worked their "fingers to the bone to put you through business school," and "How could you do this—after everything we did for you?"

"Breaking the mold" and subsequent consequences may be difficult in these situations. We fear becoming an outcast from the culture or society that brought us into the world—shunned and not accepted back. So, instead, we settle for the good of the whole to keep the peace. We put off our dreams until there is a better time to "break the news," until we have saved enough money, until the kids are out of the house, until someone dies, or until the holidays are over. We go on silently dishonoring ourselves, blaming outside circumstances and other people for our misery. Our good intentions to someday follow our hearts' desires float

> But we all have a *Nashville* (any strong cultural influence—a town, a family, a relationship, a career, an inner belief system, a clique of friends, or any of these combined) that we use to overlook what we truly desire, settling for the status quo because everyone else seems to be making it work just fine.

around in our minds until we bury them with the justifications of "I can't," "it's impossible," "I should," and "if only."

We go to the movies and identify with characters who remind us of ourselves.

By remaining in our drama loops, we suppress our intuitive voice and creative thought.

When they get lost in their lives, we will cheer them on as they go through the process of "finding themselves." We may leave the theater thinking, "It's about time I did that for myself!" but the very next day we steamroll right back into our old patterns, dismissing our good intentions as ideas that "won't work!"

We do not want to admit to ourselves that we have made a choice, and by "not choosing" we can justify the positions we find ourselves in. Instead, we base our ideals on more trivial pursuits. We define ourselves in relation to others, our work, the cars and homes we own, and our achievements to impress people in our immediate culture. Since we are projecting ourselves out into the world in order to get approval and validation in return, a "loop" is formed around the lives we create.

When we are living inauthentically in this way, we must go outside of ourselves for this energy. "What do you think of the choices I am making?" "Look at me!" We are always seeking the answers that confirm the choices that we have made. This loop needs continuous nourishment to support itself, and since this outside validation provides us with a sense of security and self-esteem (albeit false) we are content to go along with what everyone else is doing and expecting of us in the roles we are playing. This projection is like a screenplay, full of drama because it is not of our true nature.

The people we bring into our lives are there for the sole reason of supporting this "drama loop," and we keep hoping that something outside of ourselves—like making more money, going on an expensive vacation, finding the right relationship, or becoming famous—will free us from our drama. Instead, our lives become a vicious cycle.

By virtue of living in the loop, our mental and spiritual development has been arrested and we have cut ourselves off from the true source of energy. We may even really want to change, but still believe that whatever it takes to manifest our intentions for a better life is beyond our reach.

By remaining in our drama loops, we suppress our intuitive voices and creative thoughts. The energy behind our intentions is expansive, so when we cover them up, it is with strong emotions and justifications of why we cannot follow them—this creates a great deal of tension. When we feel unsettled in our lives, we look for ways to release the tension and, like anything that is held under pressure, there will be a breaking point.

There is always a price for this inner tension, leading most people to live conflicting lives. A person may have a great marriage, but a poor relationship with money. Another may go to church, but visit strip clubs on the way home from work. Yet another may appear to have it all together, but be up to her neck in bills that she is hiding from her husband. Others may appear to have the perfect family but, when they are behind closed doors, no one communicates the truth.

Are you living some version of this path? Where do you think it will lead? Is it worth it? Do you really want to look back and say, "I wonder what my life would have been like if I had just...?"

The truth is you cannot and will not feel at peace until you live true to yourself—the time to live authentically is now. Only by living authentic lives will we be able to reach our true potential.

How can we break from inauthentic living? How can we get to the essence of who we are?

The answer is to be found in expressing ourselves through the LifeBuilder process so that we clearly see the difference between who we are and what we are doing now, to give us the benefit of perspective.

EXERCISES

Discovering your authenticity is an ongoing process of unfolding and discovering. Your LifeBuilder is designed to ask you questions. By asking yourself the same questions every day, you are planting the questions deep in your mind so that you will continue to unconsciously search for the best answer while you are doing other activities. These answers will come to you when you least expect them to, giving you the benefit of reflection the next time you look at your LifeBuilder. This will allow you to instantly recognize if the answer you provided in your LifeBuilder is in harmony with the true authentic answer for you.

Exercise 2-1 Who Am I?

Write a short paragraph answering this question: *Who am I really?* What is the answer that no one can give but you? Who are you on your absolute best days, when the world is overflowing with possibility and you feel full of life? The you who shouts to the seagulls on an empty beach and the you who sings in the shower. The unlimited, uninhibited, and ecstatic you.

Make sure that what you do for a living or the role you play in your family or social circle does not dominate this statement. Focus instead on the gift of you, the essence of your soul as it applies to every facet of your life, including family and career.

Express an unlimited viewpoint of yourself. "I am" is a power statement—begin there. For example: "I am a wonderful person with a great deal to offer the world and have found my true calling," or "I am a fantastic person...." Even if you do not believe it is true yet, say it and make it true! Boldness is imperative! Remember, "Who am I?" can also include what you think you need from others: "I love and am loved fully and completely."

You may need to write this a few times to get it the way you want it, perhaps writing about all the negative stuff that may naturally come up first to clear your mind.

EXERCISES continued

Who Am I?

I am a vibrant creative fun person

Exercise 2-2 "What Do You Do?"

You never know who you may bump into! This is to prepare you for the inevitable opportunity that is coming your way to get a raise, land a big sale, meet a key business contact or change careers. Opportunities in life come through other people and the answer to this statement carries a tremendous amount of energy.

What can you say about yourself that will excite and intrigue anyone who asks you this question—including you! Write one or two easy sentences suitable for a dinner party or business conversation.

The more familiar you are with this statement, and the more it represents who you are authentically and the more it will put you into the flow.

Come from a confident place and articulate clearly. Stay away from your job title, such as "I am a receptionist," or "I am a mechanic." Focus instead on the value you bring to your employer and the people in the company: "I make people's day brighter and better by efficiently organizing the flow of traffic in the office." Express your gifts to the world! What is the service you give? Make it exciting!

What Do You Do?

I cook, I make great creative desserts.
I set a beautiful creative place setting / table
I make people comfortable

Who Am I? Tear out perforated page #3 from the back of the book. Transfer your answers to "Who am I?" and "What do you do?" to that page. Take time to carefully select each word, only writing what is necessary. Make sure the answer can be said in fifteen seconds or less for Who Am I? And ten seconds or less for What Do You?, And that each answer comes from your heart with energy and enthusiasm. Place this perforated page with your other page in the pocket of your LifeBuilder book or a safe place until Chapter Seven. Remember to stay aware of images and quotes and ideas for your LifeBuilder that you can cut out and save too.

chapter three

Underground Thinking

"We are what we think.
All that we are arises with our thoughts.
With our thoughts, we make the world."

— BUDDHA

Have you ever
stopped to
consider the sheer number
of decisions
you make every single day?

FROM GROCERY SHOPPING, to driving, to choosing what to wear—you make a decision for every move you make and every word you speak. Each of these decisions is governed by thought, even though it may not consciously seem so.

Shortly after my car ride with Jenny, I got into two industries that were growing exponentially in a Colorado economy that was booming. I believe this was the direct result of my authentic decision to move out west and my conscious desire to succeed in business.

Six years later, in 1995, my retail stores began to struggle. It was a rude awakening to discover that working hard, having good ideas, being a good person, and having a strong family life was not enough to ensure "success." Even though we were doing a brisk business, things kept moving in the wrong direction and I found myself becoming very discontent with my life.

I kept bringing in new partners with more money, taking out more loans and even expanding the store in hopes of turning things around. Nothing I did seemed to have any impact on my bottom line and over the next two years things got worse, much worse.

Miraculously in 1997, someone gave me a copy of Louise Hay's brilliant book *You Can Heal Your Life*. Reading it inspired me to take a long look at myself and my thinking. I became aware of a current of thought residing in my mind. It was like a mountain creek running under frozen winter terrain—I couldn't see it or hear it, and yet I was standing right on top of it. I was surprised at what I discovered: that it was more like a sewer running under a major city street than a pristine drainage. The more I looked at it, the more I discovered that most of the thoughts were not even mine! They were from parents, peers, and culture—and I had accepted them rather than thinking for myself.

Underground thinking is the sum total of all the thoughts and emotions that are in your subconscious mind.

This thought-acceptance of yesteryear had programmed my subconscious mind in a certain way and was now acting like a film projector—throwing old associative memories, limiting thoughts and beliefs into the Universe and affecting my decision making on a daily basis. I needed to begin thinking for myself.

Growing up, we develop a pattern of thinking that continues to support every facet of the life we have now, including the way we react to our family members, the way we feel about money and career issues, who we attract in relationships, and the way we respond to our children when they are acting out. This mind pattern will consistently bring situations to us providing opportunities to change how we think and feel. It is in this mind pattern that your drama loops are stored.

I call this thinking *underground thinking*.

Underground thinking is the sum total of all the thoughts and emotions that are in your subconscious mind. These thoughts together are like a computer program forming a "mind pattern" that is always fully engaged with the Universe as the mental plan for your life.

One of the many thoughts I realized I had was "people with lots of money were jerks," and so while I was trying hard to succeed in business, my mind was working creatively to figure out how not to have money so that I wouldn't be a jerk. I became the nice guy who could be counted on for discounts and free service! Convinced I was attracting a loyal customer base, I was not aware of how I was impacting the bottom line. The funny thing is that I knew a few nice people who seemed to have money, but I had a different message plugged into my underground thinking, somehow.

I also discovered that I believed the success of my business determined my value as a human being, and that if the business failed then I would be a failure. I was attached to the success of the business as a way to feel successful, confident, and secure. I did not feel nor think I was worthy of financial success and yet, had you asked me, I would have told you otherwise.

These two combined beliefs were deeply woven in the mental blueprint of my thinking pattern, acting like an invisible cement anchor. I bought more inventory than we could sell, convinced that since I had made such good buying decisions we would sell it. I expanded the store, ultimately weighing down the company with too many bills, convinced that it was necessary for our market positioning. Everyone and everything in my midst was a direct result of how I was feeling about myself on a deep level, but I was unaware of it then. The business was not the problem—my thinking was.

After reading Louise Hay's book, I went on a personal crusade to change the way I thought. I began to carry around a sheet of paper in my pocket with the qualities of life I desired. Reading the list over and over throughout every day, I began saying things to myself like, "I am successful," "I am selling the business," "I am a good person," and "I am debt-free," etc. Whenever I began to panic about the conditions of my life, I would go on a walk and repeat these affirmations. I was inspired and believed I would find a solution to my problems—I shifted my energy.

This piece of paper was a LifeBuilder of sorts—perhaps an ancient forefather of my current LifeBuilder.

Indeed, our thoughts create our reality.

I ended up selling my business in short order, making room for new circumstances in my life. I had temporarily arrested the old underground thinking by placing new thoughts there. There was no way that I would have ever sold the business (or turned it around) without new supportive thinking—indeed, our thoughts create our reality.

But, I did not realize that I had not permanently changed the old programming. The piece of paper had no strong emotional anchors, nor was I inspired to stay with the practice after my life changed. It was just the thinking that got me out of a jam—it had nothing to do with a compelling New Life Vision. The practice of reading the affirmations only projected my thoughts into the Universe on a superficial level. Reality coldly hit me less than a year later when my old life patterns quickly reappeared after I stopped reading that piece of paper. It was if I had tried a new diet for a while, lost some weight, and then fell off the wagon to gain it all back in a hurry.

This is why people bounce from relationship to relationship or struggle with debt. Anyone who has fought with weight issues knows what I am talking about. One of the great challenges of the weight-loss industry is in helping people make permanent changes to their lifestyle in order to achieve success. Until there is a new pattern of thought with action to support it, the struggle will continue.

Changing your underground thinking is an unprecedented challenge, akin to un-learning how to ride a bicycle. These thought patterns are so deeply ingrained in our minds that true lasting change will take a conscious and disciplined approach to using your LifeBuilder.

I had been living my life unconsciously and I was not getting the results I wanted. Being unaware of my thinking, I was making poor choices in critical moments and then having very little memory as to how I had made them.

The power of your LifeBuilder is that it changes our underground thinking to support our New Life Vision at the root level in a fun and inspiring way.

No matter what our life is really like, we have the power to move in a new direction instead of retracing our old steps. Staying focused on an exciting New Life Vision— which may include fitting into a size 6, attracting healthy relationships, living true to ourselves in the present, being honored in front of our peers for success in sales, or being debt-free—uses the mind in a constructive way.

The power of your LifeBuilder is that it changes our underground thinking to support our New Life Vision at the root level in a fun and inspiring way. But the real source of this power is that by creating your LifeBuilder you shift the blame off other people and back toward yourself by becoming authentic again. When your thinking is harmonious with your authenticity, the results are immeasurable.

We must choose to be conscious. It is our own personal responsibility and the key to creating more desirable experiences in our lives.

The way we do this is through creating affirmations that support our authentic New Life Vision and planting them into the subconscious mind. Not off-the-cuff statements, but powerful statements that have meaning and purpose.

Before we can change, we have to change the way we think.

EXERCISES

Underground Thinking

This is the most important exercise and assignment in the book, and perhaps the most difficult and time-consuming. I suggest that you set aside at least 30 minutes of undisturbed time before you start. Underground thinking is the filter through which we experience life and it supports our drama loops. Getting to the bottom of our underground thinking is vitally important so that we can express and project a new message that supports our New Life Vision.

First, we must bring our old thoughts and emotions to the surface so that they can be acknowledged and released. Bare your soul. Write fully and from the heart. The ultimate effectiveness of your LifeBuilder is directly related to this next assignment. Please feel free to write as long as you like—you may need extra paper.

My friend, Betsy, learned from these exercises why she had been gaining weight for the last ten years despite a myriad of diets and exercise routines. When she discovered that she believed *women get heavier as they get older*, it was like a stopper being removed from the drain—the weight began to just melt away. It was the expression of this underground thinking that allowed her to create space for new thought, ultimately affecting her behavior in a natural way.

Your goal is to discover your underground thinking.

Exercise 3-1 Finish the following sentences at least five times.

No matter how hard I try, I cannot . . .

make my own decisions
feel confident about my thoughts/judgements
express myself clearly
set things right, something always goes wrong.
be strong minded.

Exercise 3-1 (continued)

I wish I could . . .

be confident of myself

be happy + creative all the time

make real money

do something fun + creative for work

be more enthusiastic about possibilities.

Exercise 3-2

Circle two categories in the following that represent the biggest challenges in your life—the issues that have been chasing you around as long as you can remember—the life situations that really need to change. Feel free to add new categories.

Marriage	Body Size	Career	School
Relationships	Self-Image	Family	Religion
Home	Financial Situation	Anger	Sadness

Self-Esteem

Exercise 3-3

Fill in the blank with each circled category from Exercise 3-2 and finish the sentence at least five times—get into the emotion behind the statement.

For example: *I have to stay in the "career" I am in because I'm not smart enough to get a new one.*

1st Category I have to stay in the _Self-Image_ I am in because . . .

I don't know how to change it
I lack the confidence to feel gd about myself.
I'm not smart enough
I have a poor memory
It's the only one I have

2nd Category I have to stay in the _Career_ I am in because . . .

I have no other money making skills
I'm too scared to try something different
I don't have the memory to learn something new
I can't take the risk of moving into something w/ income
I'm not sure what else I truly want to do.

EXERCISES continued

Exercise 3-4

Fully describe the emotion(s) that you are feeling right now concerning the issues you just wrote about or just the issues themselves

lack of self worth
depressed
sad
useless
stupid

Exercise 3-5

Describe how you feel in your physical body. Pay attention to where you feel stress, relief, pain, peace, or anxiety.

-minor headache
-sick pit in stomach
-anxiety that I may reveal something unknown

Exercise 3-6

In order to avoid dealing with _____ (category from 3-2), I usually . . . (eat ice cream, watch television, exercise . . . .)

-exercise
-watch TV, read

Exercise 3-7

Summarize your challenges, fears, feelings, tensions and coping strategies into one negative belief statement. You may need to write it several times. This is your drama loop, or limiting underground thinking.

For example: *I screw everything up—I am no good with money. Since I am no good with money, I have no control over my finances. Since I have no control over my finances, I am an idiot. Since I am an idiot, I screw everything up.*

I have no confidence in myself - I can't do anything right I feel stupid

Exercise 3-8

Cross out the negative belief statement or your drama loop in Exercise 3-7.

I screw every thing up—I am no good with money. Since I am no good with money, I have no control over my finances. Since I have no control over my finances, I am an idiot. Since I am an idiot, I screw everything up.

EXERCISES continued

Exercise 3-9

Write one new powerful belief statement by turning the negative statement of Exercise 3-7 into a positive one. In order for this to work, it must have the authentic intention of change and power behind it. Re-write it as many times as necessary to get it right. This is your New Life Affirmation.

For example: *I am creating a highly successful business. I am making sound financial and management decisions as everything develops perfectly in spiritual time, for my highest good.*

I make good choices + will be succeful in everything I do. People will come to me for advise

---

LIFEBUILDER ACTION #3

My New Life Affirmation. Take out perforated page #1 – entitled New Life Symbol again. On the bottom of that page, rewrite your New Life Affirmation (see example on page 66). Place the page back in your LifeBuilder book for assembly in Chapter Seven. The goal is to link your New Life Symbol and your New Life Affirmation together with your authentic desire for a new life experience. This will re-brand your underground thinking. Continue to look for images, etc. for your LifeBuilder.

The Power of a New Life Vision

"*Dream lofty Dreams, and as you dream, so you shall become.*
Your vision is the promise of what you shall one day be."

— JAMES ALLEN

Are you on the road
that will take you to

the life you
truly_{desire?}

THE TIPPING POINT by Malcolm Gladwell (Little, Brown & Company) is a great read that supports the core principles of *Your LifeBuilder*. It is the study of epidemics and the factors that cause things to spread quickly, like illnesses, fashion trends, or best selling books. One of Gladwell's "tipping factors"—the Power of Context—confirms that environment plays a huge role in shaping human behavior.

One of the greatest achievements of the twentieth century in New York City was the enormous reduction of crime in a very short period of time during the 1990s. A close examination of this amazing turnaround reveals that something other than shifting demographics, a slowing of drug trafficking, or the improving economy caused the crime rate to drop sharply.

The Broken Glass Theory, a hypothesis of criminologists James Q. Wilson and George Kelling, suggests that crime is contagious—that the appearance of one's environment affects human behavior, and that little things like broken windows give the impression that no one is enforcing the law.

In the case of New York, graffiti was completely removed from subway trains and the toll was strictly enforced at every entry point—over a six-year period, the subway system went from being repellent to inviting. The new clean and orderly environment was a far cry from the previous subway environment. The public responded automatically to the new and improved subway environment by committing far less crime. Changing the environment caused people to feel differently and altered their behavior.

After I sold my business in Colorado, Kate and I had our first child. Instead of adventure being a high priority, we were looking for stability and predictability. An expanding family changed our entire outlook on life, causing us to make a different set of choices. That's when we moved to Pennsylvania, to be closer to Kate's family—it seemed like the right thing to do at the time.

I soon found myself saying things like: "It's important for us to be around family with young kids" or "Pennsylvania has excellent schools." While these were true in fact, we were not being true to ourselves. These were merely statements we had come up with to justify our decision to be where we were, just like the Nashville statements. We were worried about money, and out of this fear, I took the first job opportunity that came my way. I looked at it based on the promises made for future success and possible sales bonuses, not the actual job description or salary.

Within one year, I found myself bound in red tape, office politics, and meaningless work for a wage that did not even cover our living expenses.

I was living someone else's life—totally uninspired to make any changes. All I could focus on was survival and the daily struggle of doing what was required of me. I convinced myself the world was against me and that I was a victim of my circumstances. My self-esteem was at its lowest because I was working in a job that did not suit me and the managers kept telling me about how disappointed they were with me.

The tension at the office was unbearable, so I started to look through the classifieds after work. I was not even sure that there would be anything else for me, after all, what could I possibly do?

Suddenly, I saw an advertisement that caught my eye:

Six-figure income opportunity.
Help people. Be your own boss.
Independent lifestyle.
Send resume to:
PO Box 123, City, PA 10000

No job description or company name, just a request to send a resume to a blank post office box. This ad spoke directly to my authentic desire of having a specific lifestyle. I had always wanted to earn a six-figure income, even though that was at least three times my current salary! I also loved the idea of being my own boss and having an independent lifestyle! I was intrigued enough to follow through with the action of finding out more about the opportunity, so I sent in my resume wondering if I would ever hear anything.

In less than a week, I received a telephone call from a man asking me to come to his office for an interview. I did not even ask what the job was, I was too excited and did not know if I was supposed to ask.

Amazingly, the ad was for selling life insurance! During my interview I was suddenly surrounded by people who exuded a great deal of confidence and enthusiasm about my ability to make it in the life insurance business by joining their company. It was not too long before I was signing the contract papers on a new career—ironic as it was—selling life insurance.

Believe me, I would never have sent my resume had the classified ad read:

Life Insurance
Salesperson Wanted
Send resume to:
PO Box 123, City, PA 10000

Whoever wrote the ad I answered knew that the emotional anchor of a particular way of life would be more seductive than the job description. I suspect that the company had given up on the second style of advertising many years ago, deciding to focus on the benefits of the job, rather than the actual position title. They were successful with me because they bypassed my idea of life insurance, going right for my lifestyle desires.

This compelling new lifestyle— one that you really want—will begin to magnetically and effortlessly pull you toward your new life.

But here I was—entering the life insurance business at the age of 31 because an advertisement had caught my eye. My grandfather was still employed at the age of 90 and my father at the age of 61—together they had 98 years in the life insurance business. The family cultural expectations that I had grown up with had finally caught up to me.

The significance of this story is three-fold:

First, after following through with an inauthentic decision to move to Pennsylvania because it was what we thought we should do, we thrust ourselves into the culture that supported that decision. Like Nashville, it was not about the city per se, it was about us acting in an inauthentic manner which attracted us into a stifling environment. We were highly affected by our culture after that decision, and it became increasingly difficult to see our life situation clearly.

Second, this is a testament of just how strong our social conditioning is—the fact that I was drawn to the life insurance business after years of consciously avoiding it is incredible. Amazingly, selling life insurance has played a very important role in my life.

Third, I saw the first advertisement as far more that just a career prospect. It was a New Life Vision of sorts—it had the promise of freedom, income, and service, and these were high on my value list. These elements led me to the life insurance business, while the positive strong culture of this new opportunity pulled me out of the oppressive corporate environment of my old job. I rode the vision that they held in front of me right into a new career and ultimately a new life experience, past my lifelong desire not to be in the life insurance business.

This is exactly what you need to do in creating your New Life Vision. Create the lifestyle first. This compelling new lifestyle—one that you really want—will begin to magnetically and effortlessly pull you toward your new life. It is like sending your resume to a blank post office box without any other information. How the space is filled in between where you are now and the New Life Vision you create may not necessarily be known to you now. This is planning by creating spiritual awareness.

This is a choice.

To the degree that you are able to express this New Life Vision with **passion** in an extremely exciting expression of your fondest imaginings, you will increase the magnetic pull. Begin this process by accessing everything inside of you that you truly desire—anything you want to have, to hold, to believe, to experience, and to love.

Authentic desire is the catalyst for change. Without desire there is no movement. Desire disconnects you from your ruts and connects you to the wonder of what you have not yet given yourself permission to experience. Desire is your ticket to freedom and your New Life Vision is your passport—but you will only move beyond your borders if you are honest about what you want and who you are. Criticism and judgment have no place here—only positive thoughts are going to be part of your New Life Vision, nothing else.

To the degree that you are authentic in your desires—that these are truly yours without regard to anyone else's opinion or concern—you will magnify the energy of your New Life Vision and the flow of your life because the energy is being released out into the Universe rather than back into your culture for approval.

To the degree that your underground thinking supports your **authentic** passions, greater power is created because a synergy is formed. Your New Life Vision will manifest more quickly and you will find yourself in the flow. By creating your

Desire is your ticket to freedom and your New Life Vision is your passport—but you will only move beyond your borders if you are honest about what you want and who you are.

LifeBuilder, and anchoring new affirmations and power of associations, you will employ the methods of a great advertising campaign. Once this support system is in place in your mind, your life will begin to unfold naturally.

Defining your New Life Vision and expressing it in your LifeBuilder is the equivalent of cleaning the graffiti off the subway trains. A new mental environment supporting your new vision will be created and will signal your mind that you will no longer condone living a life contrary to the one you desire.

Formulating a clear New Life Vision is the first step to bringing it into reality. This expression is the catalyst that starts the flow of energy. There is great power in giving language and substance to your intentions and goals, breathing life into the change you desire. Once you dive into the realm of imagination, everything is possible. You can accomplish anything that you can picture in your mind or find words to express.

Something magical happens when you take all of the ideas that are rolling around in your head and express them through words and images on paper. You will see them as authentic or inauthentic as they pull you out of your existing life experience into a new one. If this is not immediate, it will happen very soon!

There is no prerequisite for this New Life Vision. Maybe you want to be a better father or perhaps you want to change the world. Your vision may contain seven enormous goals or one small intention. If you are still not sure what you desire, put the following questions in your LifeBuilder, and you will know soon: "What is my true purpose in life?" "What can I do that no one else can?" "How can I serve?" And, if what *The Tipping Point* suggests is true, then the behavior that is needed to support the New Life Vision will automatically show itself.

Something magical happens when you take all of the ideas that are rolling around in your head and express them through words and images on paper.

If you think about it, a lot of people already embrace the idea of LifeBuilder. Someone who wants nothing more than to be a doctor has a pile of textbooks, the raw ambition, and the commitment to follow a strict regimen toward his or her M.D.

A musician has a songbook, a football quarterback has a playbook, and a birdwatcher has a guidebook. Each, assuming that this is what his heart guides him to do, has the clear intention and authentic thinking to support his passion.

Life is not always that simple—it is multi-faceted. You might be a doctor who wants to make time for sports, birds, and music. Or you might be a musician looking for steady employment. Whatever the case, your New Life Vision needs to encompass all of the things you desire to manifest, spiritually, materially, and physically.

Each one of us carries with us a compelling story full of passion, heartbreak, failure, and triumph. Everything you need to live a fulfilling life is inside you now—you do not need anyone or anything else to complete you, you only need to be clear about what you want for yourself.

EXERCISES

What is My New Life Vision?

Exercise 4-1 Finish these sentences ten times.

More than anything, I love to . . .

Code
ski
sew
be creative
be independent
laugh
have fun
be wealthy
have security
surprise others.

If I could do anything (anything!) I would . . .

have my own business
have money to give to others
have a flexible job
do something creative for money
have fun
go away more w/ Derek
stop complaining
learn to skate
have more confidence in myself
quit nursing

Exercise 4-2

Look at your New Life Affirmation (exercise 3-9 on page 52). Imagine the life that would naturally unfold for you after you embodied this new belief and it manifested in the best way possible with passion and grace.

If you could take a magic potion to create this best life, what would that life be like? What would it be like if everything you always wanted for yourself came to be, and most importantly how would you feel? Know no limitations here. This is your Declaration of Independence.

Close your eyes for five minutes and dream—see and feel every inch of this vision. This vision is your New Life Vision. Now we need to record it. Take notes by writing what comes up for you in stream of consciousness fashion—journaling continually until you get it all down. Paint a picture of this life with words. Use additional paper if necessary.

What is my New Life Vision?

Own my own company of something I creatively developed/make that others want yielding high gains. To be able to work part time. Play w/ Deryck when I want to, be able to excercise + stay in good shape. To make something that makes other happy but not time consuming. Have money to build onto + improve our home - Be able to give freely to local fundraisers, To ski w/ greater confidence. To be able to go back to visit family at will.

Exercise 4-3

Circle up to seven of the following categories to represent the most important elements of your life or your New Life Vision from exercise 4-2. Create new categories if needed.

Appearance, Business, Career, Children, Creativity, Education, Fame, Reputation, Family, Health, Helpful People, Intimacy, Knowledge, Marriage, Mental Stimulation, Philanthropy, Physical, Profession, Relationships, Success, Sex, Spirituality, Teachings, Travel, Quality, Peaceful, Intuition, Values, Loving, Income, Thankfulness, Wealth, Soul, Confidence, Enrichment, Expression, Organization, Learning, Service, Open-Heartedness, Abundance, Joyful Living, Adventure, Self-Care, Home, Acceptance, Blessings, Harmony, Receiving, Generosity, Self-Image, Occupation, Other (specify)

Turn each category you circled above into a short goal or an intention. Some may need a couple of additional words for clarification. Keep them very short—three words or less. These will become the building blocks for your New Life Vision. Stay as open-ended as possible so that you do not limit the Universe in fulfilling your request. For example: "Abundance" rather than a specific net worth goal; "Excellent Shape" rather than a specific weight goal.

Unleashing creativity   Endless income

Successful business   Self Confidence

Unlimited success   Great Self-image

Travel at will

Your LifeBuilder | **66**

MY NEW LIFE SYMBOL

My business and my income are increasing exponentially.
Everything I need and desire is provided for me.

I am at the right place at the right time.

MY NEW LIFE VISION

Abundance
Open Heart
Creativity
Intimacy
Joyful Living
Self Care
Adventure

LIFEBUILDER ACTION #4

My New Life Vision. Tear out perforated page #4 from the back of the book. Create a list of your Seven Goals/ Intentions on this page. You will more fully express each component in the next chapter. Place this page in your LifeBuilder book for assembly in Chapter Seven.

chapter five

Advertise Your Life

---

*"Any picture held firmly in any mind, in any form,
is bound to come forth. That is the great, unchanging
Universal Law that, when we cooperate with it
intelligently, makes us absolute masters of the
conditions and situations in our lives."*

— JOHN MCDONALD
MESSAGE OF A MASTER

Why do companies in
this country spend
billions
of dollars
on advertising
every year?

ACCORDING TO A MAJOR WEEKLY NEWS MAGAZINE, the average American sees over 3,000 advertisements each day. In fact, for $20,000 a week, a company on the East Coast will continuously imprint an ad in the sand on a busy beach by towing a heavy roller with a tractor! There is no escape!

Answer—advertising works.

Your LifeBuilder works, in part, because advertising works! By creating your own self-directed advertising campaign—your LifeBuilder—and "selling" your New Life Vision to yourself, you impact your state of mind on a deep level, engaging its power to help you manifest the life you desire.

Advertising is a seductive spiral, continuously evolving and revolving around the concept that people believe what they see and hear just because it is brought to them by someone or something they either respect and admire, or have opened themselves up to—regardless of there being any validity to the material.

It has been said many times that our beliefs shape our worlds.

Never before in the history of humanity has the mind been pulled in so many directions by so many effective uses of media. With a constant barrage of news, information, and advertising in our culture today, most of us are unconsciously going right along for the ride. We read the paper over breakfast, listen to commercial radio as we commute to and from work, surf the Internet during the day, and then come home to the television at night. Somehow, most of us stand by the conviction that the media doesn't affect us—but of course it does! Infiltrating our

Your LifeBuilder works because advertising works!

belief system through our five senses, advertising weakens the power of the mind to stay focused on ourselves even though we try to stay highly sensitive, taking conscious responsibility for what we allow in.

The advertiser's goal is simple:

Anchor the image and feeling of owning the product in the consumer's subconscious mind to affect his thinking as he makes buying decisions.

The advertiser could choose just to create awareness by simply alerting the target audience to the product or service being offered.

Have you ever test-driven a new car—let's call it a blue Jeep—and been totally excited at the prospect of owning it? Not only did you like the way it looked and the way it drove, but you believed the Jeep really suited you well, and besides there were not a lot of them on the road. Then the day you drove that car off the lot, you began to see blue Jeeps everywhere, even the guy next door had one! Likewise, any newly expectant mother suddenly notices pregnant women everywhere she goes, even though there seemed to be none before.

There were not suddenly more blue Jeeps on the road or babies in the world. What happened was that your attention became focused on babies and blue Jeeps as a result of your mind being conditioned to see them. Your perception had changed, causing you to simply become more aware of those things you want or of opportunities you are looking for.

Awareness is an important first step for any successful ad campaign, but it's limited in scope. Advertisers know that they must go beyond awareness to make their prospective clients salivate for their products by branding the benefit of owning their product in the minds of their clients. Once this benefit is branded into your subconscious, it affects your underground thinking.

The first research into branding was done in 1904 by Ivan Pavlov. The story of Pavlov rubbing meat paste onto the tongue of a dog while simultaneously ringing a bell is now famous. After repeated experimentation, the dog associated the taste of meat with the sound of the bell to such an extent that he would salivate whenever he heard the bell. There are three keys to implanting this kind of associative memory:

Anchoring   Pavlov used an anchor already present in the mind of the dog—dogs love meat.

Consistency   Pavlov never rang the bell without offering food. His goal was always the same.

Repetition   Pavlov did this experiment with a great deal of frequency.

How does this tie into your **one action** and your **one habit**?[1]

Taking your one action—developing your LifeBuilder—you must express what you truly want out of life using things that you are truly passionate about, based on the anchors already present in your mind. This is your authenticity, and it is creatively expressed in your New Life Vision using powerful words and images in your LifeBuilder. This creates spiritual awareness and readies your mind to accept new affirmations in support of your New Life Vision—allowing you to see the path you must take, and could not see before.

Developing the one habit projects your New Life Vision out into the Universe. First, just the action of reading your LifeBuilder does this, but secondly and far more importantly, you are resetting your mind at a deep level with new associative memories. New anchors must always accompany the new thinking you want to embed into your subconscious mind, so that when you see the symbol of your new life, or even think about your new life, your mind associates the new images and feelings.

[1] Williams, Roy H. *Secret Formulas of the Wizard Ads*. Austin: Bard Press, 1999.

You may not even be in the presence of your LifeBuilder or its symbol, but your New Life Vision will present itself to you in ways that will boggle your mind, consistently affecting all your decision-making.

Advertisers reach us exactly the same way!

Let's look at the favorite theme of major beer commercials targeting men ages 18–34. Using the anchor that men want women, advertisers consistently place beer in the presence of attractive women accompanied by men having a great time. While these ads may change, there is always a sexual theme—*consistency*—and we see them over and over again—*repetition*.

The ultimate goal of the commercial is for you walk into the beer store thinking about having a good time and automatically buying the exact product you saw on television. The attractive woman has been removed, but by now your mind associates having a good time with a specific brand of beer. Billions of dollars are spent with the intention of getting you emotionally involved to the point of "having to have" a specific product to satisfy your desires.

After I had expanded my LifeBuilder from one photo of the mountains to many photographs, closely resembling an advertisement with colored graphics and affirmations, I began to have more fantastic experiences directly related to the emotional anchors I created for myself.

One of my favorite things in the world to do is to surf, although I had only surfed once prior to making my first LifeBuilder. I placed a large photograph of a person surfing a perfect wave next to the goal of increasing my sales. My thought was that I would link the idea of surfing (something I was passionate about) with my goal of increasing my sales. I was using the image of the surfer on the wave to inspire me to make more money!

In addition, I had another page in my LifeBuilder that had a hammock with a person resting in it to inspire me to feel more relaxed about my life. In the photograph, the sun was setting just over the ocean behind the person in the hammock. Under the image, I had written the word *Peace*.

Six months later, after looking at my LifeBuilder every day, I made a large life insurance sale that put more money in the bank than I ever had in my entire life. After depositing the check, I went to meet a prospective client for lunch and was stood up. I ate alone, and as I headed for my car, I noticed that I had parked next to a travel agency. I went in and asked the woman if she could help me arrange a trip to the South Carolina seashore for my family. She smiled at me and said, "I'm sorry, we only do international travel." I looked around realizing that it was, in fact, an international destination resort agency, so I stood up to leave.

"Well, what do you like to do?" she asked, as I was about to walk out the door.

I thought for a moment. "Surf!" I said, "do you book any of that?"

"No, I've never booked any surfing trips, but by coincidence we did just receive a fax a few minutes ago that you might be interested in—I was going to throw it out."

The fax was from a surfing camp in Zihuatenejo, Mexico! We looked at the website—the photographs were fantastic and it wasn't very expensive—it was perfect! I called Kate and bought a ticket on the spot for a four-day trip by myself the next month, despite the salesperson being uneasy about me going to a surf camp with no way of confirming it was safe, reliable, or clean.

Was this a fluke coincidence?

Well, it could have been luck, but what happened after I got to Mexico convinced me that this was no happenstance. I rented a Jeep at the airport and arrived at the surf camp just as the sun was setting over the Pacific Ocean. There was only one vacant bungalow left and it just so happened to be the only one right on the beach. I walked closer and a strange sense of excitement came over me as I spied the hammock on the porch of my bungalow. All of a sudden, time seemed to stand still. I had the sense that I was walking directly into a scene from my LifeBuilder! The surroundings were so incredible, I took my camera out of my backpack to capture the hammock on the porch of my bungalow with the sunset and beach in the background.

When I returned home I took my film to be developed immediately! I then went to my LifeBuilder to confirm my suspicions—and there it was, the photograph from a magazine of a hammock on the beach with the sun setting directly behind it over the Pacific Ocean!

I had done it again!

Amazingly, the two photos were almost identical even down to the shape and color of the hammock—the only real difference was that my hammock had no one resting in it.

I had essentially advertised to myself what I wanted and then it was all orchestrated for me.

Somehow my LifeBuilder had impacted my subconscious mind enough to inspire me to make that trip happen—and take that picture as I first arrived! I had reached both goals: increasing my sales and finding peace. Not only did I feel relaxed, I felt alive!

I had essentially advertised to myself what I wanted and then it was all orchestrated for me. I had done enough research on my target audience—ME—to know what I really wanted, and had expressed it into my New Life Vision. The vision was then associated to specific images, inspiring me to look at the book often enough to embed it into my subconscious mind. The *anchoring*. All of the goals and intentions expressed were working together in the common theme to create a better life for myself—consistency. I had created in my LifeBuilder a collection of stimulating photographs and words that I was inspired to review every workday of the week. *Repetition*.

My LifeBuilder had all the components of a highly successful advertising campaign. Does advertising work? Yes!

There is one intangible element that every advertiser strives to achieve. Trust. The ultimate goal of the advertiser is to gain your trust. Advertisers know that if you do not believe in the integrity of what they are offering, despite making you aware of fantastic benefits using solid emotional anchors, the advertising message will fall on deaf ears. They also know that once they have gained your trust advertising will not be necessary.

You are responsible for believing in your own advertising program—your LifeBuilder. Not believing will produce nothing!

I do not question anything contained in my *LifeBuilder* as I review it each morning. Instead, I allow myself to be carried away by the experiences. By not questioning my goals, and following through with my daily practice, I have no other recourse but to create opportunities like that surfing trip!

This is what you must do! Get away from being ordinary and regular! Quit dismissing your dreams and yourself as something less than fantastic. You are an extraordinary person, with desirable gifts and talents.

In your own LifeBuilder campaign, you must get beyond your conscious mind and your intellect and tap into the subconscious. The only way to do this effectively is to design something extraordinary! Use strong emotional anchors. Project the line of thinking that supports the highest new vision of your authentic self. Only then are you going to be able to produce the attitude, opportunities, and experiences you truly desire. The depth of your conviction and commitment to this advertising campaign, as well as the frequency and consistency of your participation, will create the space to let this new life experience flow.

Anything is possible if you simply believe. Inexplicable forces are working on our behalf, and developing your LifeBuilder engages you in the process of co-creation.

Perhaps at this stage of the game you are asking a few questions ....

- What if I do not know what I want—how can I express nothing?

- How do I know if I am authentic?

- How will my LifeBuilder put me in touch with the blueprint for my life?

Your LifeBuilder works because advertising works—but not in the traditional way you might expect. In the next chapter you will learn about remaining open, and having real faith and humility.

EXERCISES

Imagine that you are the executive of a brand new, potentially large advertising account. This account could make your entire career.

Your first step is learning about the clients and finding out from them where they really want to go. "What is the vision of your company?" "What are the goals that you want us to project for you?"

Your sole mission is to extract from your clients the essential facts and feelings of what their vision is for the company so that you can design an advertising campaign that really captures the essence of them. This is the account that could take you to the top!

This account is you.

Your sole mission is to extract from yourself the essence of each category in your New Life Vision into the exact best words in the form of affirmations or belief statements.

Exercise 5-1 New Life Vision Affirmations

Write the goals and/or intentions from exercise 4-3 on the short top lines on the next page. Below each one, write a new definitive affirmation statement in the present tense. This statement will be your new supporting thinking for each component of your New Life Vision. Your mind knows the life you truly desire and rather than express the entire vision here, you are capturing its essence. This allows Spirit to help you fall in with a master plan for your life that may be difficult to see fully or clearly now.

For example:

Abundance
I effortlessly attract all the wealth I need and desire, earning at least $100,000 annually.

Excellent Health
I have perfect health and enjoy exercise and a healthy diet.

Relationships
I attract people into my life who possess the values of honesty and integrity.

EXERCISES continued

Exercise 5-1 (continued)

There are hundreds of these statements on www.yourlifebuilder.com.

1. _____

   _____

2. _____

   _____

3. _____

   _____

4. _____

   _____

5. _____

   _____

6. _____

   _____

7. _____

   _____

Exercise 5-2—Ongoing

Find and cut out your images
(advertising content)

Gather up all the magazines you have lying around the house and/or buy some magazines you love. The best place to go is a huge bookstore with hundreds of selections (many of these stores throw away un-sold magazines that you can recycle for them). Look for visuals that represent your passions. Travel, real estate, spiritual, and outdoor magazines are excellent for quality pictures and advertisements.

Your goal is to find 1–10 images for each segment of your New Life Vision from Exercise 5-1. Full pages are great of mountain vistas, ocean views and patterned backgrounds, etc.

These are your emotional anchors. Look for pictures and words that make you feel good—the ocean, gardens, interiors of homes, animals, mountains, or perhaps a perfectly manicured golf green. The images must represent the fulfillment of each intention and/or goal, or just make you feel good looking at them. You may also use your own artwork or that of a friend.

Consider text like "You Deserve It" and the corresponding graphics from a magazine's advertising pages. These advertisers are professionals—use what they have produced for your benefit.

Pick out several photographs of yourself, your family, and/or close friends (if appropriate!). You must get a good feeling when you look at them. Lots of smiles!

For those who want to do an electronic version of *LifeBuilder*, just surf the web for images that excite you and save them to your hard drive.

EXERCISES continued

LIFEBUILDER
ACTION # 5

New Life Vision Goals/Intentions. Tear out the next seven perforated pages in the back of the book, entitled NLV (1-7). Transfer each of the affirmations and goals and/or intentions from exercise 5-1 onto the individual pages. Each perforated page will get one goal or intention with the supporting affirmation underneath. Place each of these pages in your LifeBuilder book until Chapter Seven. Also continue to collect all the images, photographs and artwork in your LifeBuilder book.

chapter six

Spirit Is Higher Than Intellect

"Spirit has placed a dream in your heart for a better world, starting with your family, extending to your work, community, country and stretching beyond your nation. Speak your truth and inspire others, for you are meant to make a significant and sizable difference."

**— REV. MARY MANIN MORRISSEY
LIVING ENRICHMENT CENTER**

How do
miracles
occur?

HOW, WHEN, AND WHERE YOU LEAST EXPECT!

Traditional advertising targets specific demographics with anticipated results—and you should have similar expectations. However, the key to your LifeBuilder is to be open for the Universe's interpretation of your intentions and goals.

Remember, you are targeting yourself. While the success of an advertising company may be linked to their ability to be in touch with the latest fashion trend or even having enough money to buy a Super Bowl advertisement—your success cannot be defined in such trivial ways.

You must *not* expect to receive exactly what you ask for, instead, stay open for miracles and you will receive your highest good.

In May of 2001, nine months after I had moved my family to Boulder, I looked back at the remarkable string of events that occurred in such a short time period. I had grown my insurance business by over 400%, becoming a leader in sales in life insurance for a prestigious company. I had the miraculous experiences with the photographs of the mountains and the surfing trip in Mexico. I was sure that I had discovered the magic formula and had a firm grip on how things were coming to fruition in my life. In fact, it seemed that everything in my LifeBuilder was coming true.

It soon became clear to me that this miracle had a twist.

Just moments before I walked out on stage in front of nearly 10,000 people to receive an award for my achievement as a national leading life insurance producer in my peer group, I noticed that I was trying to "fit in" with the other award winners backstage. Trying to be accepted was an uncomfortable, awkward yet familiar feeling for me.

As I waited behind the curtain, thoughts about the actual circumstances of my life, as well as the miraculous events that led up to that moment, were swirling in my mind. These two things were in stark contrast to one another as I tried to suppress the negative with the positive. As I looked into the eyes of the other award recipients, I imagined that I was inferior to them and that their lives were far more complete. As I tried to participate in their conversations about how smoothly they ran their businesses and what they were doing to sell even more insurance the next year, I began to think that perhaps I really did not want to be in the insurance business after all—I felt invisible and lost.

For the previous several weeks, I had been anticipating the glory of the experience at hand. I had called everyone in my family to invite them to Milwaukee for the grand event. I even called childhood friends and clients—anyone who would listen. I discovered later that I was putting a lot of pressure on this experience to fill a void in my life and I was still seeking outside approval. I wanted everyone to tell me that I was okay, that my professional choice was a solid one, and that I was finally "good enough." I was stuck in that old drama loop. The true irony being that I needed reassurance at the exact moment I was being rewarded for my success!

A few months earlier, just after returning from the Mexico surf trip, my name had suddenly appeared on the monthly Top 20 Sales Report. I immediately updated my LifeBuilder to incorporate the idea of being a leader in my peer group. I said to myself, "What have I to lose—let's see if this LifeBuilder thing really works." I calculated the sales figures I thought I needed to be a leader, based on what the others were producing, and recorded that number as a goal in my LifeBuilder.

Every day I drew up my prospect list on the dry-erase board in my office and tallied the insurance premium dollars I expected each would bring. My clients and I were benefiting enormously from my efforts—one sale after another began to materialize, and I was selling to the high-caliber people who had always eluded me before. Everything was working in my favor.

Concurrently I was buying new clothes and going on vacations with my family. These were not ordinary clothes or vacations—the idea that *in order to be successful, I must look successful* was the thinking that influenced these decisions (the same old drama loop). I wasn't concerned with paying off my credit cards. Why bother when the money was rolling in? I figured I would be rich soon enough, so I bought lots of life insurance and mutual funds, all according to my projections and backed by my LifeBuilder. I hired a second full-time assistant and two professional coaches. I was buying computers, Palm Pilots, and talking on my cell phone non-stop to anyone who would listen about all the great things that were happening in my life! I even led a seminar on how to be successful for the young agents in my company.

Although I was highly unaware of it at the time, I was also seeking my father's approval, just as I had done throughout my entire life—by aiming to be honored by the insurance company we both worked for. I was focused on the significance of the event rather than what was truly authentic for me.

As the year was drawing to a close, I realized that I was going to be short—way short—of my goal. On the very last day, as I was driving down the highway, I jammed my fist into the sunroof of my car, smashing it but not my hand. It was a surreal moment as I forged ahead to the last appointment before my vacation at the end of the year. I was so tired from running so hard that I almost called to cancel because this prospective client had already told me "no" so many times before. I didn't really expect him to buy anything—this was a courtesy call to a man who made a lot of money. Not ever being one to back down on a commitment, especially with such an important prospect, I went despite the fact that I had given up—there was no chance of a sale being made and I was not going to reach my goal. I felt like a failure, despite my successes.

The premium he wanted was the exact amount I needed to total the amount I had put in my LifeBuilder book two months before to win the sales award!

I was selling whole life insurance, which is rarely an easy sale—especially if you are working with people who have a hardened predisposition toward not liking any insurance. The product may be exactly what they need but getting them to take action is another thing entirely.

Frank was one of these people. He was a self-made entrepreneur. Through a successful franchise bid, he had guaranteed himself financial independence for eternity, and he HATED insurance. His total aversion for the product in general completely clouded his thinking on life insurance and he enjoyed telling me so in an intimidating fashion.

But something was different on this day. Frank looked me right in the eye and told me that he wanted to get started right away on a large amount of life insurance, one of the larger sales in my local firm's recent history. I tried not to act surprised, for in front of me was the "King of No!" Somehow I managed to pull out the application and get started.

The premium he wanted was the exact amount I needed to total the amount I had put in my LifeBuilder book two months before to win the sales award!

There was one problem. Frank and his wife didn't have time to see the doctor for the medical exam for at least a week, meaning the business would have to wait until after I was back from my vacation and the year was over. So, with application and check in hand, I thanked Frank and left his office, promising that my office would be in touch to make the necessary arrangements.

Thrilled with the sale on one hand and accepting defeat on the other, I was completely unprepared for what happened next. As I walked toward my car, Frank yelled to me and invited me to stay for lunch. Since my workday was finished, I accepted. I made myself at home in the conference room until lunch was ready and called my assistant, Mindi.

A few moments later, Frank appeared at the conference room door visibly upset, yelling, "What in the hell is going on here? I just bought some insurance five minutes ago and I have a doctor calling me to schedule a medical exam already!"

I stammered, thinking I was losing the sale; "Sorry, Frank, I was just processing the request, I had no idea that they would call you so quickly." I had, in fact, not even mentioned to Mindi to put a rush on it. She had merely put the order in because it was the right thing to do.

"I told them what I told you! I can't do it for at least a week!"

Where the words came from to respond to this statement, I will never know. Frank had always tried to intimidate me and this was one of those occasions. Normally I would have weakly said "sorry," but instead I heard myself say, "Hey Frank, what is stopping you from doing it today?"

Silence permeated the room for a moment. Then, all I could hear was the pounding of a sudden downpour that showed no signs of letting up. Frank walked to the window, looked out and sighed, "Well, I was going to play golf this afternoon—what the hell, maybe I will do it today."

Minutes before I had walked into his office defeated, now I had a golden opportunity. It was almost as if my LifeBuilder goal had materialized out of thin air right in front of my eyes. I called Mindi and she had the doctor's office call Frank back. He and his wife completed the medical exam that afternoon by driving over an hour each way. The next day we submitted the business, completing a week that most insurance agents would be proud to call a year, and I went on vacation knowing that I would be on stage a few months later.

> It was almost as if my LifeBuilder goal had materialized out of thin air right in front of my eyes.

And so here I was backstage, two months later, suddenly feeling awkward in the presence of so many life insurance people. I had spent the majority of my commission dollars expanding my business, just like I had done with the snowboard shop ten years earlier—which was a problem because Frank had just informed my office that he had changed his mind and wanted his money back. My father was sitting in the front row of the auditorium with the rest of my family, despite the fact that he did not seem to want to be there.

As soon as the glory of this weekend was over, I would have to go back home and face the real truth.

In the beginning, my LifeBuilder was only about finding outward success and achievement. I had no idea that it would ultimately be about finding myself—I did not even know what that meant.

"Gold Award—E. Dan Smith III" came over the public address system and the stage manager pushed me through the curtain. I quickly placed an all-star grin on my face and walked gracefully out onto the monstrous stage of the Milwaukee Civic Arena as thousands of people cheered. It was just like I had imagined it so many times before—it was impossible to see individual faces but it was also impossible to ignore the crowd. I paused for a moment between the two gigantic video screens on either side on the stage, gave a little wave to the crowd, and then joined my family in the front row—*exactly the same man I had always been.*

Getting the award had been meaningless—my life was no different than it had ever been. I was still looking outside of myself for my personal validation—to awards and others' praise. I was still trying to impress upon people my significance so that they would tell me that I was okay.

My LifeBuilder practice had given me everything I had asked for—and then some.

The momentum of trying to get onstage was gone, and it had given me nothing in return. I had essentially achieved my goal but my life still felt empty. I had poured so much energy into that experience, certain that it was going to be more than it was.

Realizing the truth of why I felt awkward backstage, I fired my coaches and my new assistant, and canceled my expensive life insurance policies. I sold my mutual funds and cut back on expenses. The illusion had been shattered.

In the beginning, my LifeBuilder was only about finding outward success and achievement. I had no idea that it would ultimately be about finding myself. I did not even know what that meant. I had used my LifeBuilder to achieve goals that left me feeling empty and confused. But my apparent failure had somehow strengthened me and something else was happening in my life, although I could not place a finger on exactly what it was.

As the world seemingly collapsed around me over the next several months, I earnestly studied the circumstances of my life and what had caused me to feel so unfulfilled. Recognizing that I had been in this place before, many times in fact, I was tired of the game—keeping up appearances, holding together a complicated financial debt management system, and working in a job for the outward success and approval it would bring me from my father and my peers.

As this realization began to unfold and sink in, Kate and I began living a more joyful life. I laughed more and appreciated my marriage and friendships on a deeper level. I took my little girl to school twice a week. I was not in a hurry any more. I meditated daily and deepened my spiritual practice with yoga and journaling. I woke up with love in my heart instead of frantic energy to rush into the day. Despite the fact that I had never written a book and seemingly did not have the money in the bank in order to do it, I suddenly had the urge to write, going against the conventional wisdom of trying to reestablish myself as a top life insurance producer. Some people began to tell me, in a negative way, that I had changed—but I was no longer interested in their opinions.

It became apparent to me that my world was not collapsing at all; in fact it was coming together for a much more authentic purpose. I was actually in-line with several neglected priorities in my LifeBuilder—having honest relation-ships with members of my family, being fulfilled in my life's work, having posi-

I learned that LifeBuilder was bringing everything into my life that I had been asking for—it just took me some time to realize that the way things showed up was different than I had imagined.

tive self-esteem, and making a difference in the lives of others. I learned that LifeBuilder was bringing everything into my life that I had been asking for—it just took me some time to realize that the way things showed up was different than I had imagined.

As I let go of my drama loop, newness came into my life. I stopped trying to impress people by buying clothes to look and feel good. I finally understood my father's reluctance to get excited about the award. I realized that he knew what I was going through; he loved me for who I was, not who I was on stage.

You will find your authentic life or it will find you.

Suddenly, my income and spending were curbed in a dramatic way. I learned that the fear I had been carrying around for my entire life about money was unwarranted and unnecessary. I began to notice all the majesty in living simply and being more true to myself. Amazingly, the whole time I had been moving in one direction, Spirit was working tirelessly in another direction in order to help me find my place. I was truly fulfilled by what I had been asking for all along and my peace was coming to me from a place I could never have imagined for myself.

You will find your authentic life or it will find you. You will think you are lost—in the wrong place and at the wrong time—and in that moment of confusion, if you are paying attention, you will realize that you are in the right place at exactly the right time. Spirit will guide you. Take your place and realize your importance. Celebrate your gifts, talents, and unique significance. You already have all you need to be all you desire spiritually, materially, and physically.

This will be the power of your LifeBuilder.

Let go of the anxiety and stress of your daily life. Let go of the idea that you have to control things or do everything all alone and then things will fall magically into place. Trust that you are supported by something much greater than yourself. Use your LifeBuilder to identify your authentic intentions and focus your thinking on a new vision. Faith in this process and detachment to the outcome expands us into the spiritual realm. It opens a channel of fulfillment that naturally filters out the incongruence in your life plan, helping you find your place.

None of what was happening in my life was an accident. I had reviewed my

LifeBuilder daily for over a year, following through with action and purpose, actively surrendering to what came my way. I chose to go with the flow, rather than against it. Amazingly, I was selling enough insurance to support myself with one-tenth of the effort, and I had the time to write this book.

I could still be living in that drama loop, but that road did not go anywhere near where I truly wanted to be. I could finally see that my life was pretty damn good already and that everything I had experienced was a necessity to get me to where I was now! I truly believed that all the people and things I needed to support me were in their places waiting for me to recognize them.

My LifeBuilder and the supporting practice helped me consciously choose to create a different energy in my life.

The act of looking for your life is only the beginning. Whether or not you are ready to recognize the truth is the only decision there is to make.

EXERCISES

Miracles Happen & I Believe. Tear out perforated page #2 from the back of the book. Write on that page from the place inside of you that believes in miracles or simply leave it blank for your own creative interpretation for later. You may want to include a prayer. Place this page in your LifeBuilder book. In the next chapter, you will begin to put together your LifeBuilder.

chapter seven

Crafting Your Lifebuilder

"What we see we think, what we think
we imagine, what we imagine becomes."

— ERNEST HOLMES
SCIENCE OF MIND

It's time to make
a powerful
statement about who you are
and what you want
out of life.

AS I HAVE ALLUDED TO EARLIER, this is the final part of the one action—the assembly of your LifeBuilder.

Oh, how tempting it is to resist this stage. Somehow, people are compelled to come this far and not follow through—as if this book is really about reading and nothing else. This book is about creating *your* book—now.

> "Until one is committed, there is hesitance, the chance to draw back, always ineffectiveness. Concerning all acts of initiative (and creation), there is one elementary truth, the ignorance of which kills countless ideas and splendid plans: that the moment one definitely commits oneself then Providence moves too. All sorts of things occur to help one that would never otherwise have occurred. A whole stream of events issues from the decision, raising in one's favor all manner of unforeseen incidents and meetings and material assistance, which no man would have dreamt could have come his way. I have learned a deep respect for one of Goethe's couplets: "Whatever you can do, or dream you can, begin it! Boldness has genius, magic, and power in it. Begin it now!"
>
> — from *The Scottish Himalayan Expedition*, by W. H. Murray

I wish there was some measurable way to communicate what will happen as a result of putting your book together, but I am convinced that it is far too mystical for our own understanding. But something does happen in the creative process that is extraordinary by bringing the following elements together:

Faith—The simple act of completing this book is a tremendous act of faith. Essentially you are communicating to yourself that you believe in yourself as well as some inexplicable force that will ally with your efforts. You know that by creating your LifeBuilder you can create the life of your dreams.

Commitment—The message of committing to the process goes deep into your being. This is a far cry from setting a New Year's resolution or making a wish on your birthday. This is a much larger commitment, and you can feel it.

Reflection—After you have your LifeBuilder in physical form, you will gain new insight into many areas of your life, including your thinking and desires. What is most amazing is that you will immediately gain the benefit of hindsight. You will recognize things in your book as being either outdated or inauthentic; since you no longer need them, take them out of your book. When you do this, you essentially remove them from your life. Very powerful.

Frances held back for months before finally making her LifeBuilder. It happened rather suddenly—she announced that she was going to stay home and put her book together minutes before her family was going on a group trip. So off they went without her. It was a great weekend for her. When her family got back to house on Sunday, she showed them her LifeBuilder—it was extraordinary. She had stayed up almost the entire Saturday night getting it just right.

Immediately, her life began to open up in an unexpected way. Frances has never been one to be interested in the theater, but one of her pages was entitled "Creative Expression." I think her idea of creative expression was more in terms of oil and canvas because she had done a little of that. Nevertheless, it was not long before she was performing a one-woman theatrical show for her women's group. They liked it so much that they recommended she formally produce it, and she did. More amazing than the actual experience was what she learned about herself by doing it.

It never would have crossed her mind had she not placed "Creative Expression" in her LifeBuilder.

Another woman, Susan, called the day after she made her book to say that she had just sold her house that day after putting a "Sold" sign next to a photograph of her house in her LifeBuilder. It was only on the market for one day.

Get ready, because something just as miraculous is going to happen in your life now.

As you begin constructing your LifeBuilder, it is paramount that you are in a positive frame of mind. If you want a new life experience then you must access a parallel level of thinking. I highly suggest that you set time aside, away from the distractions of the busy part of your life, and create a nourishing atmosphere for yourself with healthy food, a comforting environment, plenty of sleep, and a great deal of peace.

Take time to craft your LifeBuilder. Remember that the quality of energy generated every day in your LifeBuilder practice is directly related to the content of the book you create. Choose every image and every word carefully and, above all else, make sure that your book will motivate you to pick it up again and again.

There is no right or wrong—just put in what feels authentic to you. As you develop your practice, you will naturally know when something just does not feel right anymore and remove it. You will always be updating your LifeBuilder. My original LifeBuilder book looks nothing like the one I have currently, but it has always been about being true to myself and helping others.

Get ready, because something just as miraculous is going to happen in your life now.

While I am providing you a template for making your LifeBuilder, I highly urge you to be spontaneous. Please use your own creativity and intuition as you develop your book. Use a computer or a paintbrush, whatever feels the best to you. I suggest stretching your imagination and using lots of color. Utilize technology and make it as fancy as Madison Avenue would right from your desktop, or choose a more organic approach with longhand and glue. Whatever you do, keep each individual element congruent with the whole theme and let your uniqueness flow onto the pages!

Fill your LifeBuilder with content that you love, in the same way that you use your heart in choosing which pictures to place around your home. The amount of passion with which you create your LifeBuilder directly corresponds to the life changes you will make!

One of the most important aspects of your LifeBuilder is that it will ask you questions that your mind will answer while you are asleep, in the shower, or on the way to the grocery. Engage with these questions each time you read your book and you will influence your mind to think new things.

Create your LifeBuilder pages or "life advertisements."

Except for your New Life Symbol, (perforated page 1), each of the perforated pages you have completed represents two pages of your LifeBuilder book, the first being the page itself and the second open for your creative interpretation.

In other words, when your book is laying open, you should only be able to see one aspect of your LifeBuilder. We have provided one-page examples for your benefit after these instructions.

You will need:
- Your LifeBuilder book
- All the perforated pages completed to date
- Blank white 8.5" x 11" paper
- Your images, photographs and artwork, and a myriad of supplies (glue, scissors, stapler, markers, etc.)

(If you want to make an electronic LifeBuilder, go directly to our website and click on *LifeBuilder Help* for more suggestions. My recommendation is that you create the book first. Then, after you understand LifeBuilder better, consider the electronic version as a supplement. It is more powerful to create it first with your hands.)

How to create the first LifeBuilder page

1. Take out your LifeBuilder book and retrieve the perforated page entitled "My New Life Symbol."

2. Either attach My New Life Symbol or transfer the symbol itself to a blank piece of paper or the LifeBuilder template, so that it will be the right size to fit into your LifeBuilder. The template is available on www.yourlifebuilder.com.

3. Put your creative stamp on this page to make it compelling. It will be the first page you look at daily. This page should be fairly simple so you can use it in other places.

4. Insert My New Life Symbol into the first clear page of your LifeBuilder book so that it is the first page you see when you open your book.

How to create the rest of the LifeBuilder pages

1. Turn the most recently completed page of your LifeBuilder to the left. You should now be looking at a blank sheet of paper on the left, and nothing on the right. Retrieve the next perforated page (they are numbered at the bottom right corner).

2. Either attach the perforated page or transfer its information to a blank piece of paper and lay it on the table in front of you to the left.

3. On the right, take a second blank sheet of paper and lay it on the table so that the two are side by side.

4. Take your images, photographs, and artwork, and create a two-page advertisement (see "Art Direction," page 102). You will want everything to be solidly attached to each page.

5. Insert the completed pages into the clear plastic pages so that when your book is laying open, you see both pages side by side.

6. Repeat until you finish the book. See the examples on page 103 and/or go to *www.yourlifebuilder.com* for *LifeBuilder Help*.

Art direction

Each page can simply have the background of one shade of color or pattern, or may be an extensive collage. But each page ought to be compelling enough to change the way you feel when you look at it. Choose your images, colors, and words to be displayed in the same way an art gallery might.

Focus each intention/goal page on the positive aspects of that intention or goal—what life feels like when this has been realized. If you desire to lose weight, fill the page with what life will be like when you are thinner—the new wardrobe, the new relationships, and the increased energy you will feel. Or simply associate images and colors that speak to you.

The main goal is to make the life you want to live come alive in a visual format with feeling. Create an ad campaign for your own life as if it were airing during the Super Bowl.

I keep seeing LifeBuilder books ranging from professional businesslike, generated from the computer using very traditional lettering with highly specific content, to those that are artistic in nature—collages complete with melted wax, tin foil, black and white photos, herbs and perfume, and other highly creative materials. Some have completely broken the mold—with few or no words using only color and no images. Whatever you feel will help make it attractive to you, feel comfortable doing it! Some have even included "the 100 things I want to do before I die" page. If you want to add pages, go ahead.

Order of LifeBuilder pages

1. Symbol / New Life Affirmation

2. Miracles Happen & I Believe

3. Who Am I? / What Do You Do?

4. My New Life Vision & List of Goals / Intentions

5–11. Affirmation Statement Pages (up to seven)

These pages are from chapters that follow:

ADVENTURE

"I have plenty of money, time and resources for fun adventures."

for Sure

FREEDOM

OH BEAUTIFUL

Take a Deep Breath

So now that you have made Your LifeBuilder, what next?

Privacy—keep the contents of your LifeBuilder to yourself

The only reason you would want to show it to anyone else is to get his or her opinion. The only reason you need anyone else's opinion of anything you do is if you do not trust your own. If you do not trust your own, then you have lost faith—the cornerstone of your LifeBuilder.

You will be tested many times on this issue. People are going to want to know how you are changing your life and you will want to show them. Also, in order to validate what you have placed inside your LifeBuilder, you will seek another's opinion. Perhaps you'll get lucky and the person you show it to will say: "Wow, this is terrific; I believe that you will get the life you desire and more!" But, if they are not at least this supportive, it will cast a shadow of doubt about your LifeBuilder intentions, weakening your resolve and belief.

The general rule would be that if you need to ask somebody his or her opinion about the contents of your LifeBuilder, it is not authentically representing you and you need to take the contents in question out.

Nurture and protect the life of your dreams—guard it as one of your most sacred possessions and do not dilute its power by opening it up for interpretation.

There is one exception to the privacy rule: Choose one strong person or a group of strong people who are actively using LifeBuilder—only they can unconditionally support your LifeBuilder. This is not about having someone else validate your intentions or showing off your book, but allowing room for a trusting relationship to help you to go deeper. Listen to what your heart says about the ways in which you can enhance your book when you show it to this person or group.

For example, Kate and I routinely share our books with one another, but we do not pull them out for guests, unless they are intimate friends who are actively working with LifeBuilder.

In the next chapter, there are detailed instructions about how to set up a LifeBuilder practice and LifeBuilder Focus Group.

Practice

Throughout the ages, spiritual traditions have used prayer, ritual, and mantras—mystical formulas of invocation or incantation—to help people strengthen their minds, become more disciplined in their thinking, and remain open to spiritual growth. In a similar way, daily practice with your LifeBuilder can help support a new way of being in the world—it will strengthen your mind. How you show up will affect your results, and it is your results that are creating your new reality.

Now that you have completed the one action, it is time to begin to explore the one habit:

Practice.

Chapter eight

Setting
Sail

"Get busy living, or get busy dying."

— ANDY DUFRESNE
IN THE MOVIE *THE SHAWSHANK REDEMPTION*
BASED ON THE BOOK BY STEPHEN KING

What are you waiting for?

IN THE FANTASTIC MOVIE *THE SHAWSHANK REDEMPTION*, Andy Dufresne (Tim Robbins) is serving a life sentence in Shawshank State Prison for a crime he did not commit. While all the other prisoners talk of being institutionalized, Andy focuses instead on the inner freedom inherent in all human beings: "… there are places in the world that aren't made out of stone, there is something inside that they can't get to, that they can't touch. It's yours."

He often speaks of getting out of prison someday and maintains the vision of going to Zihuatenejo, Mexico, and operating a charter fishing boat. He keeps this positive attitude despite the hopelessness of his situation and the downtrodden attitude of his fellow inmates.

Even his best friend, Ellis "Red" Redding (Morgan Freeman), counsels Andy on the danger of being hopeful about his situation. "Let me tell you something my friend. Hope is a dangerous thing. Hope can drive a man insane. It's got no use on the inside. Better get used to that idea." Red is convinced that even if his parole was approved, he wouldn't make it in the "outside world" because of the years of conditioning imposed upon him by prison life.

Have you become institutionalized? Is your thinking cemented in a way that it would keep you from making it in the "outside world"—the world of your dreams? Have you bought into the myth that hope is a dangerous thing? Do you even believe your dreams are possible?

Red is unwilling to have faith because he does not want to be disappointed. He figures that the status quo is far better than falling short of his dreams or failing, so he becomes a successful inmate. Andy's response to Red's fear about "making it on the outside" is to say, "I guess it comes down to a simple choice, really. Get busy living or get busy dying."

Andy sees stars out his prison window while Red only sees the bars. Andy's exciting and inspiring vision of a better life is the catalyst that propels him to take the action necessary to attempt to transform his mental image into his physical life. His desire for leading fishing trips off the western coast of Mexico is a very strong magnet pulling at his very being. He is vigilant about his dream despite the negative cultural pressures around him.

Somehow, in the face of the culture in which we live, we have to imagine a better life and be willing to do whatever it takes to attain it.

You have to make the same choice. Solidly hold your New Life Vision in your mind as strong as Andy does—that vision must motivate you to do what is necessary to escape from your own mental prison. Believe that the content of your LifeBuilder already exists in the world—all you must do is remain open to endless possibility, and follow through.

How to Use your LifeBuilder—the one habit

1. **Develop and practice a daily ritual.** This is the repetition, repetition, repetition segment of your self-directed life advertising campaign. Immersed in your New Life Vision, you will create the space and the energy necessary for it to manifest.

2. **Create a supportive culture.** In order sustain a practice with new thoughts and actions, you will need to make some significant changes in your internal and external environments.

3. **Take action!** This is the physical activity that you must take to bring your New Life Vision into its form. You must put the pen to the paper and the

shovel to the dirt, without hesitation. It is time to act now!

The Ritual

It was Ralph Waldo Emerson who said, "Nothing great has ever been created without enthusiasm."

There is power and energy in the Universe—you cannot see it, nor can you escape it—but you can experience it and revel in the results of its awesome power. To connect with it, to get into the flow, you must go to its level.

Developing a practice and maintaining it over time will anchor your New Life Vision in your mind as it replaces your old limiting thoughts and beliefs with new supportive ones.

You must become enthusiastic about the content of your LifeBuilder. You must get into a higher level of thinking by accessing your subconscious mind so you can change your underground thinking and access the spiritual realm.

Developing a practice and maintaining it over time will anchor your New Life Vision in your mind as it replaces your old limiting thoughts and beliefs with new supportive ones. Be patient with yourself—this will not be easy or instantaneous. Do not be at the mercy of expecting instant gratification.

Change your interior environment first and then the exterior will begin to change in support of what you desire, at exactly the right speed for you. You are replacing a pattern of thinking that has been formulated over decades—it takes time. It's like going full speed across the ocean in an oil tanker and then suddenly realizing that you need to go in another direction. Changing course can be an immediate decision, but it will take quite some time for the tanker to turn 180 degrees and reach full steam ahead again. While some parts of your thinking will quickly lose their influence, other thought patterns will take longer, perhaps much longer to change.

This posture is difficult to hold. We are accustomed to going on the latest and greatest diet and making New Year's resolutions.

What I am suggesting is very different: reviewing your LifeBuilder every day will instill a new line of thinking over time that will loosen the effectiveness of the old underground thinking. Your life will begin to change as your new behavior naturally aligns with your thinking.

Prepare your mind and develop a ritual—Integrate a ritual that has significance for you. Strive for the most direct communion with whichever forces you believe to be supporting you in your process. Before you review your LifeBuilder, take at least five minutes to get yourself in the right frame of mind. Ideally, you will do this after exercise, stretching, writing, meditation, painting—anything that joins your mind, body, and spirit together. Not only will this open your awareness, but it will also send the signal that you are ready to begin.

I suggest you review your LifeBuilder for 10–20 minutes, five days a week, in the same place and at the same time each morning, and then a quick review at night just before bed. Keep this date with yourself and create a space for privacy. A consistent practice will build on the energy of each previous day, helping you build momentum; you will naturally become more receptive by maintaining a routine.

Make the time—Let go of the excuse "I really don't have time"—it can always be directly translated into "I really don't care." If you are ready to care enough, this will be an appointment you can easily keep. Look at what you do in the morning and replace one thing: reading the newspaper, sleeping late, or catching up with friends. By devoting this time to yourself, you will begin creating balance and boundaries in your life. Just after waking is the best time to read your LifeBuilder because your mind is still in the Alpha state, making it more receptive, but you must create the time in your day when you know you will continually commit.

Read your LifeBuilder out loud cover to cover—Really! Read it with great emotion to anchor your New Life Vision. You need to hear these words and your mind will respond just as objectively as if someone else were saying them—there is no difference. Be animated; create whatever energy you need to hear. Vividly imagine the actual feeling and experience of all that you desire. Conjure up all the elements of your New Life Vision and replace negative thoughts with positive ones.

This is NOT about living in a fantasyland; it's about creating in the present moment. In the evening, I recommend a more meditative approach. Read your book silently and concentrate more on impressing the words and feelings into your mind. As you are falling asleep, let the words and images flash across the screen of your mind.

Professional application—When I was using my LifeBuilder to boost my business, I kept my book at the office and focused it on what I needed to be successful. You may choose to take this approach. Practicing your LifeBuilder ritual at the office first thing in the morning will provide you with the confidence and energy to improve your relationships with people responsible for making buying decisions or management changes. I have provided a special *LifeBuilder Business* section on the website, under *LifeBuilder Help*.

Pace yourself—Disconnect from needing to know how everything is happening behind the scenes, and patiently witness your life evolve into an authentic expression of your true nature. Think of your practice as an organic way to allow things to naturally spring forth. Changes may take a great deal of time; know that you have all the time you need. If you want to lose weight, getting on the scale seventeen times a day is exactly the opposite approach to take—throw it away instead. Summon your new thinking; let go and live.

Carry *LifeBuilder* with you—Or at least keep a symbol of your book with you for a quick reminder during the day. Relying on how powerful logos are in corporate America—and in the same way that many people put affirmations on mirrors, in the car, or on their computers—and keeping your LifeBuilder logo in these same places and your mind will immediately be able to access your New Life Vision.

Keep a notepad handy—You will notice changes that you want to make during your ritual. Pay attention to your feelings and record new ideas of what to include or aspects to eliminate. Trust your intuition completely and write these down so you can update later. Expect your LifeBuilder to be in a constant state of flux reflecting the movement and action in your life.

Update—Your LifeBuilder will go stale quickly without revisions. When you lose the motivation to look at your book, it's time to update the contents—this is essential. In time, you will discover that much of what you thought was important enough to be placed in your LifeBuilder doesn't really belong. Make room for the inspiring aspects of your New Life Vision that need to go in. The minute you record something new, you allow yourself to see things differently. Every time you see or hear something of significance, immediately put it into your LifeBuilder. Keep the nuggets of gold and get rid of everything else. Personalize your approach to your LifeBuilder and let the layout shift if it needs to in order to accommodate changes.

Take LifeBuilder vacations—If you take this practice too seriously, you will burn out and lose your perspective. Take time away from your routine; this will happen naturally and will always lead to new insights.

Use your other senses—Listen to a special CD, light a certain candle, or add perfume to your book. Anytime you want to invoke your LifeBuilder, just play the same CD, light the candle, or wear the perfume to access all that it contains.

Quiet the mind—Learn to be quiet with yourself and take the time to listen—this is when the questions in your LifeBuilder will be answered. Most of the time it seems as if everyone and everything is grabbing at us for attention. It's up to you to focus that attention inward from time to time. Spend some quiet time with yourself so that you can hear what your intuition is trying to tell you. Become conscious of the amount of television, radio, gossip, Internet, and newspapers you let into your life every day—try journaling, meditation or walking instead. It is so easy to go right for the TV, radio, cell phone or newspaper, always having some kind of background noise or activity.

THE BOTTOM LINE—I designed a LifeBuilder practice that suits me, you will have to find what works for you. You may want to have some aspects of your book on an altar in your home, in a collage on the wall, or hanging from the rearview mirror in your car. Maybe you want a waterproof book for the shower! Make your practice part of your life in any way that works for you!

Create a Supportive Culture

Since our culture plays such a significant role in supporting our thinking and activity, it will be necessary to make some changes as you move deeper into your LifeBuilder practice. It's important to go slow and easy, integrating changes as you are inspired to.

Create "**An Inner Circle**" to secure the encouragement and support of others to follow through on your New Life Vision. This may include hiring a LifeBuilder coach or developing your practice with your partner. Knowing that others are following through on their practice will help you to hold yourself accountable to your own.

LifeBuilder Focus Group

You can also form a **LifeBuilder Focus Group** of like-minded people who meet once or twice a month. Here are some guidelines that may help you:

The purpose of the group is to create a LifeBuilder experience that is exponentially more powerful than anyone could achieve on his or her own. The energy from these meetings will help everyone maintain an individual practice while receiving new insights into the contents of his or her LifeBuilder book and his or her lives.

– *The group should consist of at least three people.* Four is the ideal number for group dynamics and seven is the maximum number. For married couples or partnerships I suggest bringing in more people, but a balanced relationship can be a group unto itself.

– *Everyone must be positive.* It is imperative to keep harmony in the group by choosing people who will not sit around complaining about their hard lives rather than moving forward with New Life Visions. We know how other people's negativity can bring us down and the group dynamic you create is directly related to the energy of each individual person—one person can destroy the harmony of the entire group.

— *Choose a facilitator.* Designate someone who will make sure that the focus of the group remains positive and solution-oriented.

— *Everyone participates fully.* Start each meeting with a brief sharing time so that everyone can update one another with his or her LifeBuilder miracle stories to get the energy flowing.

— *Everyone brings one challenge.* Each person brings to the group one life challenge he or she has within his or her LifeBuilder. While this may be emotionally difficult, it is not a time to complain or criticize. Instead, it is a time of expectancy, understanding that this challenge is really an opportunity in disguise and will be resolved soon. It is critical that all the members of the group hold a sacred space for the person speaking, listening intently.

After sharing this challenge and revealing the corresponding pages of their LifeBuilders, the group members now listen only as other members respond. As a means of support, each member offers one idea for "Going to the Edge"—an action to move through fear and confront life head on! Most of the time we do not allow ourselves to see what we need to do, but others can often provide the means for turning a challenge into an opportunity. The group then holds each other accountable for one specific activity that brings them to their Edges—facing that which you have not allowed yourself to see.

— *Drama loops.* The group is to listen for underground thinking and belief statements supporting each member's drama loops and/or negative patterns. This is the most powerful part of your relationship to the group because of how liberating it is for someone to finally understand exactly what thoughts or beliefs she or he needs to let go of to move forward.

— *Statement of gratitude.* Each person gives a statement of gratitude for the miraculous changes that are occurring to bring his New Life Vision into his life. I encourage each group to organically create a closing ritual that feels right.

There is always a reason why what is in your LifeBuilder is not coming to pass. While we usually explain these away, the focus group holds up a mirror so that we can plainly see our responsibility and the corresponding action that needs to happen, and then holds us accountable for "Going to the Edge."

Clean up your physical environment

Is your external environment in conflict with the life vision you are projecting? Do you need to replace that 25-year-old dirty lime-green shag carpet with a shiny new hardwood floor? Everything around you will affect what's inside of you. I have felt tremendous energy shifts after cleaning out my car, painting a room, or aligning the environment of my home with the principles of Feng Shui. Not only are you responsible for creating the life you want to live, you are responsible for creating the space you want to live it in!

Action

While this book's focus is primarily on creating new mental space and energy for a New Life Vision to manifest by creating your LifeBuilder and following through with a supporting ritual, you cannot co-create without going into further action. While to some it may seem that I am stating the obvious, it is clear to me that most of us feel a lot of fear when it comes to actually following through. It is my intention that this book will dispel a lot of those fears, and you will more naturally spring into action being inspired by reading your LifeBuilder book, but I decided to dedicate a little space to action anyway because most of us resist doing what we need to do!

My philosophy is that the motivation to go into action is purely supported by what we are thinking. I've noticed in my life that when I was doing what I loved to do, I never had trouble following through on those things that needed to get done. This does not mean that following through was always easy, but when it involved something that I was passionate about or believed would happen, strict accountability was not necessary.

When you find it difficult to follow through because of fear, you have exposed your underground thinking (again).

When we find harmony with our thinking, our authenticity, and our New Life Visions, things just work out—through being in the flow.

In the summer of 2001, I watched my five-year-old daughter go through an experience that sums up how I feel about going into action.

Eliza and I were standing on our porch watching the neighbors get ready for a garage sale. They suggested to Eliza that she set up a lemonade stand and take advantage of the customer traffic on a hot day. Eliza had seen other kids in the neighborhood doing this and she thought it was a great idea, so we went to the store to buy the necessary supplies.

We mixed the lemonade, made a sign, and set up a table right across from the garage sale easily enough. But I noticed that the closer we got to finishing our preparations, the more nervous she became. She found out that thinking about selling lemonade was very different from actually selling lemonade! It took some coaxing to help her follow through with what she had started.

When her first customer arrived, she was so nervous that she literally sat there frozen, gripping my leg and looking at the ground. In fact, the whole process had turned my outgoing and confident child into a scared rabbit. We all laughed at her shyness, causing her to become even more withdrawn.

The next customer began to coach her by showing her how to pour the lemonade and how the money worked. Soon there were more customers who wanted to help the little girl with the initiative to set up a lemonade stand. She was getting the hang of it—enjoying her renewed independence—so I decided to go inside for a while.

I returned to discover that she had recruited a few of the neighborhood kids to help her. They had developed a system of collecting the money, making the lemonade, and pouring it all by themselves.

"Daddy! Daddy! Guess what? Look at all this money!" She was so proud of this major accomplishment and I was thoroughly impressed at her transformation into a young businessperson.

Despite her fears, she learned what she needed to and leapt right into action, and she attracted the right culture of friends and customers to help her run the stand. She had seen other kids do it successfully so she knew it was possible, and she willingly accepted the help of others.

Eliza found the courage to put herself out there to see what would happen—so can you! The Universe will automatically respond to your activity just like adults do when they see an enterprising kid behind a lemonade stand! You will be supported in your endeavors by people, healing energy, money, ideas, solutions, etc.

Remember:
No matter how hard you want to grip someone's leg in fear,
action is holy and the Universe will respond to the quality of your action.

Action will cause many mental and physical changes in your life—some will happen immediately and others will take much longer. Your new outlook will only last as long as your passion is deep, your practice is consistent, and your culture is supportive. Your activity will stir up pockets of resistance to moving forward. This resistance is merely what is currently between you and the life experience you desire—embrace it and stick with it!

EXERCISES

Exercise 8-1 ## Supporting Events

The purpose of Supporting Events is to plant in your mind how you expect things *might* come to pass. These are specific action affirmations representing what you are going to do and what you expect to happen in support of your New Life Vision.

For example, you might write: *I am getting a raise, or, I am meeting my life partner, or I am meeting the right people to help me build my new business, or I live in my dream home, or My income is increasing, etc ....*

These Action Affirmations are very important. Be conscious that they may change more than any other aspect of your book and that they should not be limiting, using open-ended language like *at least* with <u>no</u> specific dates.

Write up to seven supporting events—they need to be clearly identified.

EXERCISES continued

Exercise 8-2

Design your LifeBuilder practice:

I intend to review my LifeBuilder book _____ days per week,

on the following days _____,

at this time _____,

and in this place _____,

for at least this amount of time _____.

Exercise 8-3

Write a letter of commitment to yourself about your new daily LifeBuilder practice. The letter must include the details of your practice and WHY you are doing it and some statement of faith.

For example:

Today I start a new life, one of expectancy, excitement, enthusiasm, and self-care, because of my new commitment to myself to open up to the life that I deserve to live.

I am committed to the following ....

The reason I am committed to this practice is because ....

I believe that my practice will allow ....

_____

_____

_____

_____

_____

_____

_____

Exercise 8-4

Send us a copy of your commitment from exercise 8-3, and we will keep it in a sacred place for you. After a period of time, we will mail it back to you so you can see how much your life has changed. These will remain private! Email to: *committed@yourlifebuilder.com* or mail to: P.O. Box 19726, Boulder, CO 80308-2726.

Supporting Events. Tear out perforated page #12 from the back of the book. Write your Supporting Events on that page or on an 8.5" x 11" sheet. Create a two-page "advertisement" and place it in the next open pages of your LifeBuilder book.

My Major Goal. *(optional)* Tear out perforated page #13 from the back of the book. Make one spread of your LifeBuilder book dedicated to a major specific goal. This goal can be a part of your New Life Vision or something new. This has worked so many times for me! Write out your goal in detailed language and then illustrate it. If it is a home you desire then describe it in perfect detail, including the number of rooms you want, etc. Capture the feeling of the goal—not just the goal itself. I have written checks to myself when I wanted to increase my income, designed the "sold" sign for my home on paper when I wanted to move, drawn the ribbons I wanted to wear at the next sales meeting for awards, and placed photographs or names of people I wanted to meet—all in my LifeBuilder. Place it in the next two open pages of your LifeBuilder.

chapter nine

High Seas!

---

*"We must free ourselves of the
hope that the sea will ever rest.
We must learn to sail in high winds.
It is during our darkest moments that
we must focus to see the light."*

— ARISTOTLE ONASSIS

What lies between

you and
your destiny?

ABSOLUTELY NOTHING—NOTHING PHYSICAL THAT IS.

Everything between you and your New Life Vision is either a thought or an emotion. As you fully embrace your LifeBuilder practice and go into action, you will be exposed to many forms of this energy—positive and negative.

The positive energy is the natural pull of the Universe engaging you in a new direction, supporting your authenticity. Once you set it in motion, you will reach many LifeBuilder goals quickly and easily. You will be in the flow.

The negative energy is your mental resistance to new activity—your underground thinking keeping you locked in a comfort zone. The motion created by your practice has brought it to your attention. This energy may cause you to want to stop using your LifeBuilder so that you do not have to face your fears or negative emotions.

It is important to understand that both the negative and the positive energy are necessary for completing the new mental and spiritual circuitry that you seek.

Imagine that you began the construction of a dam on a river when you were born. As a result, a large lake was formed to cover up what was once a pristine valley. The environment was slowly altered over many years and the locals who lived near the lake became accustomed to it as a part of their lives. New people moved near the lake, enjoying the recreational activities it offered.

You are the river that has been sectioned off into a lake. You have now decided to remove the dam and drain the lake. Imagine what will be revealed when the water is let out: trash, decomposed trees, dead fish, rocks with algae, and a lot of mud. Also imagine the reaction from all the people who had become attached to the lake as it was.

Your social conditioning during your formative years was akin to building that dam and blocking the flow of the river. The public opposition to draining the lake represents the resistance you will experience from your friends and family as you try to change. Returning the valley to its original natural habitat is the fulfillment of your New Life Vision.

Exposed at the bottom of the lake you will discover the natural consequence of your social conditioning, including limiting beliefs and suppressed emotions. In order to attain what you desire, you will have let the river flow freely and be willing to "clean up" what has been buried. What was hidden from your view underwater was part of your underground thinking, much of it placed there as a natural protective mechanism when you were young.

Letting all the water out at once will "flood" you with overwhelming emotions and thoughts. What may add to this difficult task is that what is exposed will be from a different era, long buried under water, making it unrecognizable and perhaps painful to experience again. As this happens, you will have to resist the natural temptation of re-damming the river by reconciling the old with the new in order to move forward.

This will be the true test of your practice; as you cleanse yourself of what no longer works in your life, you may find that friends who seemed to support you in the past are not interested in the new you.

My friend Jack has a page in his LifeBuilder that states, "I am in good health, taking excellent care of my mind, body, and spirit." He quit smoking cigarettes as a part of his LifeBuilder practice. He used to think his cigarette cravings were just a "bad habit," justifying them as something he "did with the boys," thinking that he "could put them down anytime."

His search to find out the true cause of his cravings led him to discover that his longings for sugar and nicotine went well beyond the physiological—they were emotional—and that he was unconsciously covering up his suppressed emotions and thoughts about himself in regard with these vices.

In a world of change, there must be gain and loss.

Through his LifeBuilder practice, he began to experience himself as totally healthy rather than just focusing on quitting smoking and junk food. He was rehearsing in his mind how his day would proceed without cigarettes, actually creating the space for health, and he was able to plant the seed of intention in his mind for the dream to become reality.

In addition, he discovered how to release the emotional blocks that were in his way by becoming a "witness" to them, rather than a participant. "At first, I felt so fragmented," he said about himself during this period, "like I did not know who I was," as all the buried emotions surfaced. But he learned that there was a moment in which he could make a conscious decision to either go with what he had rehearsed in his practice or revert to old behavior. He chose to make a change.

He also discovered the truth of his immediate culture. His friends were not interested in supporting the changes. They wanted him to stay the same—to keep smoking and justify their own decisions. He learned that his social life had been undeniably influenced by the unconscious desire to stay away from his thoughts and justify his own behavior. For a period he tried to hang on to his new practice *and* his old friends, thinking that he needed them somehow. But it was in the experience of letting them go that he found new friends and soon discovered he did not miss the old culture or the old habit.

In a world of change, there must be gain and loss.

By quitting smoking, getting into shape, getting out of debt, getting out of a difficult relationship, losing weight, or dealing with any significant change, you expose the thinking that supported those life choices. These thoughts are the true obstacles to authentic self-expression; removing them causes your shadow to be exposed. You can either embrace it or run from this truth. The paradox is that running away always leads you right back to what you wanted to avoid.

Here we must make the choice to recognize this as the gateway to spiritual growth—the great opportunity to live authentically. To do this, we must have the faith that Spirit is working with us to lead us in the right direction. We cannot expect to circumvent these issues, but to honestly see them for what they are, just thoughts and emotions that we can let flow through us when we no longer need them. Hardly anybody wants to admit having a tough time and no one wants to talk about it! People in this culture, men especially, are seen as "wimps" for allowing these emotions to surface, and yet it is only repressing these emotions, hardened by decades of hard cultural conditioning, that is in the way of us living authentically.

Here are some suggestions for staying afloat in high seas:

• Persistent practice—keep asking for what you want over and over again.

• Deepen a supporting spiritual practice.

• Release the need to be defined by your negative thoughts and emotions.

• Seek the help of a supportive community.

• Give your body the energy it needs to help you process your emotions and relieve stress—find something physical that you love to do and do it.

• Do something wonderful for someone else—donate time or donate money to a charity, give flowers to a dear friend, cook dinner for your partner.

• Effort and strain are not necessary—stay open and let go in order to create the space for new experiences.

This brings us to the completion of the expression / projection / action cycle first mentioned in the Introduction. The first part of the cycle is expression. You have expressed the old and limiting underground thoughts and emotions to get to an authentic expression of your New Life Vision, which is now creatively expressed in your LifeBuilder. Though projection of your New Life Vision, through a supporting LifeBuilder ritual or practice, you will be inspired to follow through with action, both the action of creating a supportive culture and the physical activity necessary for manifestation.

This will cause High Seas! Once you become stifled and are no longer taking the necessary steps toward your New Life Vision or reading your LifeBuilder, then it is time to begin the cycle anew. At this stage, you will discover the next layer of limiting thoughts, beliefs, and emotions that need to be expressed, allowing you to refocus on a more authentic expression of your New Life Vision.

This is the process that will move you closer and closer to an authentic life experience. And your LifeBuilder will always be changing to stay in touch with where you are. Ultimately you will recognize—for the first time, perhaps—what you need to release. The "cutting of the cord" in Chapter Ten will set you free.

EXERCISES

Current Challenges & Questions

Challenges are really opportunities in disguise.

Challenges, like needing a little help getting the rent paid or finding love for your child when she is rebelling, arise suddenly. Or perhaps there is that one big issue that has been following you around forever, and no matter what, you cannot seem to turn it into a positive affirmation or imagine life without it.

You may feel reluctant to put these things in your LifeBuilder but there must be a page dedicated to these types of challenges so the Universe can work its magic.

Exercise 9-1

Make a list of seven or fewer current challenges in your life that you have no idea how you are going to get over or through. Pose them as questions now, to get the answers later. For example:

The following I turn over to Spirit, knowing solutions are imminent.
How can I become debt free?
How can I lose weight?
How can I find a fulfilling career?
How can I get along with my partner?

_____

_____

_____

_____

_____

_____

_____

_____

EXERCISES continued

Exercise 9-2 (optional)

Include a prayer to acknowledge that you are giving this up to the Universe and ask to be shown what you need to do, believe in, or release yourself from in order to turn the challenge into an opportunity.

_____

_____

_____

_____

_____

_____

_____

Your LifeBuilder

LIFEBUILDER ACTION # 9

Current Challenges & Questions. Tear out perforated page #14 from the back of the book or just use a new piece of paper. Write your Current Challenges on that page, along with the optional prayer. Any time you come face to face with a challenge, add it to this page of your LifeBuilder—and remove the ones you resolve. Create a one-page "advertisement" and place it in the next open pages of your LifeBuilder book.

chapter ten

Cutting
the Cord

---

*"We must be willing to get rid of
the life we've planned, so as to
have the life that is waiting for us."*

— JOSEPH CAMPBELL

What do you
need to
let go of?

EVER SINCE I MADE MY FIRST *LIFEBUILDER*, I have talked to countless people who are somehow stuck in their lives and can't see a way out. No matter what specific issue is at the core for them, they have not learned to trust themselves enough to break the mold and create lives worth living.

My mother died when I was nineteen. One of her best friends invited me over for tea and while I do not remember our exact conversation that day, I do recall her telling me that one of my mother's greatest regrets was trying too hard to fit her round peg into a square hole.

I too have tried to fit myself into a mold that did not suit me. The cycle of trying to be someone I was not and then rebelling against it has caused a lot of frustration in my life. Even though it took more than fifteen years for me to digest what my mother's friend told me, I now understand.

The nuggets of truth that we need to hear are there for us—we must be willing to listen. They may come to us at an afternoon tea, through a conversation on a subway train, from someone at the grocery store, or in a line in a movie we see. Often something will surface that we heard long ago when we are truly ready to pay attention.

I believe that on some level everyone knows when he or she is in a relationship that is not healthy. We know when we are being taken advantage of and we know when we are working solely for money and prestige instead of leading a fulfilling life. We know when we need to spend time with our family and friends even though there are so many things on our list to be done. We know that when we push people around with attitude and muscle we are really only angry with ourselves. We know that even though we are not getting caught stealing, cheating, or lying that we are weakening ourselves with every such act. We know that when we are angry at someone that we are really angry with ourselves. Perhaps we are not able to explain it, but we know when our lives are inauthentic, and that's when we need to cut the cord by replacing toxic relationships and behaviors with healthy ones.

The only thing truly holding you back from living the life of your dreams is you.

The only thing truly holding you back from living the life of your dreams is you.

Cutting the cord means accepting that we have been approaching our lives from the wrong angle—that we were mistaken. We must retrain ourselves to believe that exposing ourselves exhibits strength, not weakness. By exposing ourselves, we force growth and the courage to manifest and create new opportunities. Cutting the cord is like cutting up your credit cards when you finally admit that you are powerless to stop yourself from overspending.

It is the energy that we place outside of ourselves that we really need to redirect to co-create with Spirit from an authentic place. Only after you let the cat out of the bag and have no place to hide can the Universe take you out of your drama loop and shine the light on your authentic path.

When we do this, our energy shifts. No matter how bad we think the consequences will be for telling the truth to someone we love, it will be far better than keeping the drama loop alive.

The most empowering event of my life was cutting the cord on a mental and emotional drain that had been consuming me since I can remember. I was often possessed by this toxic energy that seemed to live in my neck and shoulders, always bearing down heavy behind my eyes. I was consumed for weeks at a time, so completely in fact that I would just retract from my life. I spent several years in traditional therapy while also seeking the help and advice from the entire spectrum of spiritual counselors. I explored religion, astrology, philosophy, and self-help but nothing seemed to work.

My antidote, of course, was to stop seeing my life through the lens of my drama loop—trying to make myself feel better by having others approve and honor me.

I wish I could say that cutting the cord was easy, but it wasn't. It took many years of self-discovery to identify the source of the cord in the first place. Moving back to Colorado was a step in the right direction. Creating my first LifeBuilder was another. But it was not until I fully developed my LifeBuilder practice, got clear on my New Life Vision, and went into serious action that I exposed the true underground thinking that was the essence of what I needed to let go. It took many cycles of expressing how I felt on the inside—through writing, talking, crying, and then projecting a redefined New Life Vision through my LifeBuilder and going into action with my practice—that I was able to distill it down to the truth. And even today I am sure there are more layers to uncover.

I told you how I felt when I returned home after being onstage—facing the reality of my life, making some changes, cutting the cord on many types of behaviors. In that space, I was able to see what needed to be done next. I carefully crafted a letter to my father, cutting the emotional cord that bound me to those behaviors. For as long as I could remember, I had blamed him for a myriad of things that had gone awry in my life and only now was I really in touch with that. I held such intense anger for what I thought he had done to me and continued to do by not approving of or accepting my life choices. What I discovered, however, was that my anger was only a disguise to protect me from having to accept the personal responsibility that being mad at him was really about being mad at myself. Blaming him was my mask for not having faith.

Somehow I knew that I had to write him a letter even though it wasn't really about him—it was about me. At first, it still carried the anger and the blame in an attempt to make him feel bad but, as my awareness shifted, the letter began to take on a different tone.

I must have rewritten that letter hundreds of times. Finally, when I was sure that it was coming from the purest and most humble, loving place, my father and I took a walk on the beach and I gave it to him. The letter pointed out the difficult parts of our relationship and identified how I thought the relationship could improve. I also reminisced about all the great gifts he had given me without blaming, only with love. There was no sugarcoating. It was a real truth-telling and it was not easy to do.

Soon afterward I realized that I was not as frustrated about parts of my life as I had been before. I could see my life from an entirely different angle. Much of what I thought was anger toward my father was really the unexpressed grief of losing my mother at such an early age. The letter actually released my anger, allowing my grief to flow through. I was no longer blaming my father and my family heritage for my problems because I had removed that option.

The energy I had been wasting on my drama loop was now available as authentic power to direct me toward new thinking, adventures, and projects. The words of this book began to spill out onto the page effortlessly. It was the best act of self-care I have ever given myself. Today, my relationship with my father is far better, and the trickle-down effect on my marriage and children is positively immeasurable.

We must believe that by exposing our hearts we will manifest new opportunities. Sometimes we must take extreme measures to break our drama loops and crack our worlds open.

We must believe that by exposing our hearts we will manifest new opportunities. Sometimes we must take extreme measures to break our drama loops and crack our worlds open.

This happens naturally through the entire *LifeBuilder* process of expression and projection. You will act until you run into the next layer of underground thinking or emotion that is standing in the way from being who you are. When you become stifled again, look for what needs to be expressed.

Everything was connected—my intention for a better life, tearing out the picture of the mountains, the inspiration to craft my first LifeBuilder, and then ultimately having everything crash around me in order to find a new life purpose in writing and teaching. Cutting the cord created an unprecedented energy shift that allowed me to focus on my true priorities by redirecting my passion, energy, talent, and love.

This is not easy to do because of the natural human desire to want to control things. While a great metamorphosis is happening, you will want to see and understand how it is all coming together. It may feel like the crumbling of your personal empire. Your old life will try to cling onto you like a spider web and you will have to keep brushing it off. Everything that once felt permanent gets washed away and you will want to hold on to what you had as a way to make sense of it all. All the emotions and feelings from which you were protecting yourself now flood your consciousness, and it is human nature to try and avoid these thoughts. You realize that everything is impermanent, yet you want to hold on to that which feels solid.

The choices you make in these moments of distress become the foundation on which you build again. While in the midst of craziness, it will seem easier to build using the materials of your drama loop. You must resist the temptation to do so by deepening your daily LifeBuilder practice, updating your book's content to reflect your most authentic expression. It is from this place that you will begin to realize that there is nothing to build—you need only recognize yourself as complete.

Once you are on your authentic path, you will see that there is no other choice. Now you will only choose to do what you love, for you know in your heart that one authentic action must lead to another. By doing what you love you keep the coincidences flowing.

There is a waiting period of surrender in a place of nothingness. "But I am supposed to ... (be in insurance!)" we scream. "Show me what you want me to do!" we scream louder.

This is the moment when we must choose between love and fear.

Recognize that when we choose love, we become super-empowered because we have allowed our intuitions to have the voices for which they were always asking. Everything changes in this moment because you realize that you are not at the end of a journey, but at the beginning.

There is no way to fail this test, because all roads lead to the same place. You will find yourself in this place again and again until you get it.

If you are looking for the starting point, you are there. Put together your LifeBuilder book. Choose anything that you love to do and begin to work with it as the central theme.

By creating your book and starting your practice, you will actively surrender yourself to your New Life Vision. By rededicating your passion, your energy, your gifts, and your love to the life you have now, you will be propelled into a new life experience. You must live your life fully and completely. The changes that manifest do not have to be as dramatic as mine in order to be significant to you. In fact, the most beautiful life transitions will be the simple ones, deepening your relationships those who matter most, including yourself.

The moment you surrender, the rest of your life will come calling.

I wish you well on your journey.

EXERCISES

Gratitude

The most ancient of all spiritual principles is to give and then receive. Since you are openly declaring your New Life Vision and expecting to receive some version of it in return, it is essential to express your gratitude for it coming to pass and offer your service.

This can be a short statement of gratitude or a long soulful prayer. The importance of this is not to be overlooked. Take the mental posture of knowing that everything you desire already exists and that the Universe is bringing it into your experience through your service. Offer gratitude for being included in the creative functions of the Universe and for being totally deserving of the gift of your life.

Exercise 10-1

Write a prayer or statement of gratitude.

EXERCISES continued

Your LifeBuilder

LIFEBUILDER ACTION # 10A

I Am Grateful. Tear out perforated page #15 from the back of the book, or just use a new piece of paper. Create your LifeBuilder page. This is one page and should be opposite of your Current Challenges page. Also, on bottom of this page, you will see **"How Can I Serve?"** Ending your LifeBuilder with one final question will keep us open to receiving more that we ever imagined.

LIFEBUILDER ACTION # 10B

Your Own Design. On the last perforated page, create a page for world peace, or any page of your own design. Alternatively, have everyone in your LifeBuilder Focus Group, business, or family, make exactly the same page dedicated to a shared intention. The influence of many people looking at the same page every day is very powerful.

Congratulations!

Your LifeBuilder is complete. I encourage you to engage with your LifeBuilder as deeply and as often as you can. Over time, you may want to add new concepts and ideas into your LifeBuilder that I did not recommend, and delete certain things that I suggested. Please let us know what works for you so that we can make it available to other people with the same desire for a better and more authentic life experience.

There is a page on our website, *www.yourlifebuilder.com*, dedicated to the sharing of miraculous changes in people's lives using *LifeBuilder* called *Miracle Rides*. Please visit to read and share often.

Thank you.

Recommended Reading

Books

Allen, Marc. *The Ten Percent Solution: Simple Steps to Improve Our Lives & Our World*. Novato: New World Library, 2002.

Gladwell, Malcolm. *The Tipping Point: How Little Things Can Make a Big Difference*, Boston, New York, London: Little, Brown and Company, 2000.

Hay, Louise. *You Can Heal Your Life*. Carlsbad: Hay House, 1999.

Holmes, Ernest. *The Basic Ideas of Science Mind*. Los Angeles: Science of Mind Publications, 1980.

McDonald, John. *The Message of a Master: A Classic Tale of Wealth, Wisdom, & the Secret of Success*. Novato: New World Library, 1933.

Williams, Roy H. *Secret Formulas of the Wizard Ads*. Austin: Bard Press, 1999.

Audio

Boland, Jack. *The Science of Goal Achieving*. Publisher unknown. www.churchof today.com

About Spiral Ranch

 The Spiral Ranch Foundation's mission is to provide people with a simple tool that will improve their lives. By living purposeful, meaningful, and authentic lives, we can each make a difference in the world.

Spiral Ranch Publishing will donate at least 10% of *Your LifeBuilder* profits towards the purchase of the Spiral Ranch Retreat Center and create the Spiral Ranch Foundation.

The Spiral Ranch Foundation is a not-for-profit corporation dedicated to bringing people together to create and share their LifeBuilders as part of a community. The Spiral Ranch Retreat Center in Colorado—in June 2002 it exists only in my mind (and of course in my LifeBuilder)—will provide the environment for like-minded people to create the lives of their dreams.

For more information about Spiral Ranch and how you can help, please visit *www.yourlifebuilder.com*.

About the Author

"E. Dan" Smith III lives in Boulder, Colorado, with his wife, Kate, and two daughters, Eliza and Ava. Since 1998, he has been a financial representative for Northwestern Mutual Financial Network, where he was recognized as a national leader of life insurance sales for his peer group in 2000-01, and honored as a convention speaker. After graduating from University of Alabama with a B.A. in Communications in 1989, he moved directly to Colorado, opening a snowboard and mountain bike store. During this time he also directed nationally televised snowboarding and mountain biking events. He has since embarked on a passionate mission to help others improve their lives.

I do make good choices and will be successful in everything I do People will come to me for advise.

WHO AM I?

I am a vibrant, creative, fun person!

[paste your photo here]

WHAT DO YOU DO?

I make great creative desserts, setting a beautiful creative table making people feel good + comfortable!

3